THE PRISON TEACHER

STORIES FROM A WOMEN'S PRISON

MIM SKINNER

SEVEN DIALS

First published as *Jailbirds* in Great Britain in 2019 by Seven Dials
This paperback edition published in 2021 by Seven Dials
An imprint of Orion Publishing Group Ltd
Carmelite House, 50 Victoria Embankment, London EC4Y 0DZ

An Hachette UK Company

10 9 8 7 6 5 4 3 2 1

Paperback ISBN: 9781841883335
Ebook ISBN: 9781841883342

Typeset by Input Data Services Ltd, Somerset

Printed and bound in Great Britain by Clays Ltd, Elcograf S.p.A.

MIX
Paper from
responsible sources
FSC www.fsc.org FSC® C104740

www.orionbooks.co.uk

This book is for those without whom it would not exist:

The amazing women who contributed to its writing and those who feature in the stories.

My brilliant colleagues who continue to work hard and love relentlessly.

And the prison service, without whose support the stories could not be told.

CONTENTS

AUTHOR'S NOTE

The contents of this book are based entirely on fact. To anonymise the individuals involved, some events and stories have been conflated and some names, descriptions and other identifying details have been changed. I am grateful to my long-suffering family and friends for lending me so many pseudonyms.

This is not a definitive manual on how to fix prisons – far from it. I want to contribute to a dialogue, I want to kick-start conversations, and I accept some of my reflections might turn out to be wrong. I'm okay with that and I hope you will be too.

It's important to keep in mind that this is an incomplete picture. I haven't included experiences of women of colour and trans men in the female prison system because I didn't see enough of them – but they are a really important part of the story that we need to be listening to. I've added a further reading list at the back of the book which includes people who have important stories to tell about their lived experience so you can build a bigger picture.

The words I've used to describe people, where relevant, are the ones they used themselves. They might not always have been the ones I'd have chosen or the ones that are the most 'woke', but I wanted to make it feel recognisable for the people in it.

And where I've lacked the relevant experience, I have consulted other people to check that things ring true: women who've been to prison, academics, prison volunteers, the LGBT+ community, mental health sufferers, and trauma and sexual assault survivors.

PROLOGUE

'The pubic hair cuttings were found after your class went on their toilet break,' Tom said pointedly, 'so it really should be *you* who calls security to report a tools breach.' Tom was the new instructor working next door. He had, like a number of other staff, come from an army career and so had a good sense of both order and hierarchy.

'I'm sorry,' I replied, protective of my small group at the same time as being fairly sure that it was one of them, 'but you have absolutely no way of telling whose hair that is. It could have been there all morning for all we know, so it just as easily could have been one of your workers.' The hair in question was a fairly standard brown – with the exception of the over-sixties, anyone could have done it. 'Besides,' I added, 'I've just counted my scissors in and we have a full set.'

'So do we,' Naomi, the other instructor replied, laughing. 'Whoever the culprit is had obviously finished.'

The bathroom housed two cubicles adorned with biro names of who loved who and the dates they had loved each other, and was attended by an almost constant tobacco hum from illicit mid-morning smokes. It was shared equally between my arts inclusion group and Naomi and Tom's 'sewing sisters'. Working in the sewing sisters was a privileged job. They made curtains and pillowcases for other prisons and were more skilled and better paid than my slightly more eclectic bunch, who were, at the time, creating papier-mâché sculptures of objects they associated with 'home' for one of our under-attended exhibitions. You also couldn't be a sewing sister if you were consistently on a behaviour report. The stack of files which arrived on the department desk at the beginning of each activities session – for instructors to write up any unruly performances of the person to which the file pertained – was almost always passed on to my classroom rather than Tom's. This meant, of course, that any department complaints were also usually directed towards us.

'Do we even need to call,' I asked, 'if the tools have all been counted back in? I'm not sure that counts as a security risk, does it?'

Naomi frowned. 'It would have done if someone cut their wrists rather than their bush.'

She made a good point. I returned to my workshop, hoping to discreetly call security after it had finished, but news had quickly spread.

'Did you find out whose the pubes were?' Jeanne asked loudly, leaning on a desk. Clearly the group's speculation around the incident had meant that work had ground to a halt on the paper-pulp police van being constructed on the Formica table. They had gathered around it, displacing an in-progress cotton-wool Big Mac while they were at it.

Jeanne continued, 'I reckon it was someone from next door. Just 'cause they're posh it doesn't mean they're not filthy.' The class nodded and whooped in agreement. 'And if it was one of us we'd have just come out with it,' she continued, as though providing conclusive proof of her theory.

'I reckon Ami,' someone else chimed in, referring to a small tanned girl whose neat eyebrows gave them cause for suspicion. 'The Polish lasses keep it tidy.'

'Okay,' I interrupted, 'can we not generalise about the Polish, even if we mean it nicely. More importantly, you've only got three more days to finish your artworks, so let's move on to a different topic, please.'

'I'm not using these if they've been round Ami's muff,' Jeanne said, handing me her pair of red-handled scissors etched with their security number.

'Fine. If you all stop mentioning Ami and pass in your

scissors, I'll wash them over lunch. And, for goodness sake, don't be tempted to give yourself a copycat trim. I realise "don't trim your pubes" isn't in the rules list but ideally it shouldn't have to be.'

'Why don't I add it to the group agreement anyway?' Jeanne said, flashing a smile.

The group agreement was a collaborative contract we'd written together at the beginning of the course. It included: 'respect one another's opinions', 'go to the loo one at a time' and 'have a go at the day's activity, even if you don't think you can do it'. The agreement had then been decorated amply with glitter and hung at our classroom's entrance for us to refer back to over the following three weeks.

'No thank you, Jeanne,' I replied, laughing. I imagined the embarrassment of having to explain the poster to a visiting security governor.

Everyone handed over their scissors and the rest of the morning's tools for me to count in before lunchtime movement was called and I let the group file out. As I was cleaning up the last of the PVA which had puddled and begun to congeal along the desks, the classroom phone rang.

'Is that creative industries? It's Jack calling from security. I hear there's been some unauthorised movement of tools this morning. Is everything accounted for?'

I'd only been in the job a couple of months and, other

than during introductory security talks, had yet to come into contact with the department.

This, it would turn out, would not be the last time.

'Oh, er, yes, it was fine, a pair of scissors went to the loo, but they came back,' I replied.

'And what happened? Did you have to call healthcare out?'

'No,' I swallowed nervously. We'd been warned in our talks about the severity of a tools slip. I picked my nails, wondering whether *I'd* have to go on behaviour report after Jack finished his investigation.

'And no tools are missing?' he continued.

'No, all accounted for. I've just signed them in.'

'Then how do you know they went to the toilet? Did you see someone take them?'

Security officers (SOs), unsurprisingly responsible for the prison's security, were the stern grandfathers of the prison family and not the types you'd make loo jokes in front of – even less likely references to 'pubes'.

'I'm afraid we found some evidence in the cubicle,' I cleared my throat. 'Some, erm, hair.'

'Hair? Christ, couldn't they just wait and put in an app for the training salon?'

I winced as I said it. 'I'm afraid it wasn't that sort of hair, sir.'

Jack went quiet. 'Right . . . well, in any case, tools should not be going out of the room. Do you count them every time someone goes to the loo or has an appointment?'

I was starting to feel a little panicked. 'No, that's not in our tools policy – we'd have to count them every ten minutes. I would spend the whole lesson collecting them in and out again.'

'You don't have to collect them in,' Jack said patiently, 'just get everyone to hold them in the air and count them when someone needs to leave the room.'

'Okay, right. I'm sorry about that. I've only been here a few months and I've not seen anyone else do that. I will from now on. Thanks for your help.'

'No problem, that's what we're here for,' Jack replied. 'And if you have any more problems, just give us a call and we're happy to come down and advise. You keep a closer eye on the tools from now on.'

I set down the phone, exhaling loudly, both in relief and incredulity before going next door to tell Naomi.

On the way out I noticed the group agreement had an addition. Between the gel pen instructions to make sure everyone has a turn to speak and not to remove artwork from the classroom without permission, it now read in blue biro, 'NO FANNY TRIMS.' I smiled at the addition and, as I often did, imagined how the challenges of that working day would compare to those of my office-based friends and family. I could whine about pay, but I could not fault the job's variety, or the creativity of my colleagues.

That afternoon, I was determined to be vigilant. 'Scissors!' I shouted for the third time in an hour, so I could count them up before allowing someone out to the loo. Begrudgingly, everyone looked under scattered newspapers for the remaining pair I needed to see before they could go.

'I'm not being funny,' Jeanne said, rolling her eyes, 'but if we have to hold our scissors in the air every time someone goes for a wee, can we not have weak-bladder-Cath in the class?'

INTRODUCTION

It goes without saying that prisons, with their locked doors and fingerprint scanners, are not exactly an open book.

We hear headlines and news reports and Jeremy Kyle's insights, of course, but rarely the individual stories of those whose lives are tangled up with the criminal justice system. And these short, sharp sound-bites mean that what we're left with is a boiled-down narrative of goodies and baddies. We just cast different people depending on which paper we like to read. It might be violent offenders, neglectful mothers and in-curable psychopaths on the one hand, or cruel officers, the evil establishment and sexist judges on the other – but, very rarely, just humans. When I started working in prisons, part of me expected to find this pantomime cast of characters. Instead I met wonderful, funny, brave and resilient people with complicated stories – on both sides of the bars. No Cruella de Vils or *Shawshank Redemption*-style officers, just Sandra, Jeanne and Officer Mark.

This book is not a piece of research diagramming the workings of the criminal justice system or Her Majesty's Prison Service. Instead, I want to take you 'inside' with me. I want to show you a little of what daily life looks like for those working and living inside, through tales and snippets from one prison, at one time, with one group of women (and a few men) – it's a small snapshot of a big system. A system which has, for too long, been one of our country's guilty secrets.

I'm so pleased to be able to include some fantastic pieces from women who've been in prison, but as it has been mostly my fingers on the keyboard, the stories are mainly from my perspectives and memories. I won't pretend to know what it is like to go to sleep every night in a shared cell, or to only be able to see your kids at an appointed pre-booked slot, but I hope these stories will amplify the voices of women in prison. They are some of the bravest people I've ever met.

It is not a book full of angelic, wrong-place-wrong-time, deferential, remorseful victims of circumstance either. I could have written that book but I would have had to miss out quite a few people. I'm not blind to the fact that you don't go to prison for doing good things, and there were lots of people we invested so much in and they chose to go back to the drugs anyway, and there were people we trusted who ultimately we shouldn't have. But have you noticed that's what we tend to do when we want to make a case for someone? Characterise them as blameless: hardworking and charming, but 'down on their luck' like Oliver Twist, as though it is behaving 'properly' which entitles people to adequate support and provision rather than deserving it by virtue of being our fellow humans. That's the mistake we made with the girls and women in the Rotherham case. We didn't fight to protect them as hard as we fight for any middle-class girls who go missing, because they didn't behave like we thought victims should – they weren't compliant, they took drugs and they went back to the perpetrators. They weren't the right type of victims.

I worked in the prison as a teacher and chaplaincy assistant for two years, and continue to work with the women I met there on the other side of the gate. Throughout my time there, I wrote in diaries and on scraps of paper most weeks to help process some of the things I saw and heard – and, by the end of my time there, because it was homework set by my counsellor. I never expected these scraps to end up in a book. But the more I've sat round dinner tables and told stories of my work and the people there, the more people have responded, 'I can't believe it! How come more people don't know about this?'

Criminal justice isn't a niche interest, a campaign hobby for the interested few or something you care about because you work in the industry. Crime and re-habilitation affects us all. What happens in prisons mat-ters. It matters because we all know the mark it leaves on you or people you know when you're a victim of crime. It matters because women in prison aren't the worst people, they're typically the most vulnerable; and it matters because of the 83,430 people in prison in England and Wales,[1] 83,360 are coming out again at some point to a town near you.[2] It's not rocket science to work out that we're better off if those people become part of our society, rather than isolated from it. People are much more likely to stay in the crime cycle if they don't have a stake in a community, and positive relation-ships with people around them.

But the thing is, it's difficult to care about prisons, and

---

[1] 'UK Prison population statistics', https://researchbriefings. parliament.uk/ResearchBriefing/Summary/SN04334 (date accessed: 31/10/18).

[2] Martin Evans, 'The 70 prisoners serving whole life sentences in the UK', https://www.telegraph.co.uk/news/2016/11/25/70-prisoners-serving-whole-life-sentences-uk/ (date accessed: 31/10/18).

the people inside them, if you don't know much about them. And while there are some great policy documents and reports out there, let's be honest, most people – myself included – don't have the time or inclination to read them. Humans are, on the whole, affected more by faces than facts. David Attenborough did far more to get us interested in climate change than all the fact-packed policy documents put together. We were persuaded to give up plastic straws and walk to work not by bar charts but by his narration of footage of a small iceberg-marooned polar bear separated from its mother. And likewise, after months of news reports by foreign correspondents in 2015, the public tide on accepting refugees only really turned after a photograph was printed of the body of a child found on a Turkish beach, and we looked past the numbers and saw a boy called Alan and suddenly cared a bit more.

Now, don't get me wrong, the statistics on women's prisons are really bloody important. The charity Women in Prison found that 79 per cent of the women they work with are victims of domestic violence. Forty-eight per cent of women in prison report that they've committed crimes to support someone else's drug habit, usually a partner; 53 per cent have been victims of child abuse. These statistics paint a sad picture, where women in prison tend to be victims of more significant crimes than those they have been convicted of.[3] To top it all, in a country where under 1 per cent of children are in care, 31 per cent of the women in prison have been.[4,5]

Prison just doesn't work for women: 48 per cent of women leaving prison are back within a year. This rises to 61 per cent if the sentence was under 12 months and to 78 per cent for women who've been to prison more than 11 times.[6] Part of the problem is that most of the academic literature on prisons has, for decades, been concentrated on the male perpetrators who make up 95 per cent of prison residents.[7] We have a prison indus-

[3] Summary from Prison Reform Trust's Bromley Briefings, http://www.womeninprison.org.uk/research/key-facts.php (date accessed: 27/08/18).

[4] Summary from Prison Reform Trust's Bromley Briefings, http://www.womeninprison.org.uk/research/key-facts.php (date accessed: 27/08/18).

[5] May Bulman, 'More than half of female prisoners are victims of domestic violence, new research shows', https://www.independent.co.uk/news/uk/home-news/female-prisoners-women-prison-domestic-violence-victims-more-than-half-prison-reform-trust-report-a8089841.html (date accessed: 27/08/18).

[6] Key Facts, Women in Prison, http://www.womeninprison.org.uk/research/key-facts.php (date accessed: 15/10/18).

[7] Coleman, Almond and Manus, 'Do female offenders differ? Comparing the criminal histories of serious violent perpetrators with a control sample', www.onlinelibrary.wiley.com/doi/full/10.1002/jip.1485 (date accessed: 15/10/18).

try designed for men (which is not designed that well for them either, but that's a book for another time). It's not that we don't know these facts. Phillip Lee, former justice minister and co-author of the 'Female Offender Strategy' published in 2018, said, 'On visits to women's prisons up and down the country, I was struck by how most of the women who get caught up in our criminal justice system are among the poorest and most vulnerable.' But as Lee also notes, 'Completing the transformation [of women's prisons] depends on proper funding.'[8] It's not a secret that a traditional prison model does not work in giving the support needed to stop the reoffending cycle of women. It's a tumble dryer of victimisation, homelessness, addiction and criminalisation, not to mention the fact that more crime continues to create more victims of crimes. The trouble is, we just don't have the resources allocated, or the politicians willing to prioritise prisons, to get to the root of the problem.

But I'll stop the lecture there. As with the examples of Attenborough and Alan, I'm not going to spend the next few hundred pages listing statistics or quoting from

---

[8] Phillip Lee, 'Reforming female prisons will break the cycle of crime', https://www.theguardian.com/commentisfree/2018/jun/29/residential-centres-women-prisoners-funding (date accessed: 27/08/18).

reports. Instead, I'd love to share with you some of the stories that have shaped a journey that has made me laugh as much as it has made me cry. The journey of how I learnt, beyond a doubt, that we can't just separate off the 'evil' parts of society and think, *Hey presto! Now we can live in harmony with the moral majority.* It doesn't work like that. The line between good and evil can't be drawn either side of a custodial sentence, or across the prison threshold, or between area, class, gender, religion, nationalities or profession. It runs right through the middle of every human heart. And who is willing to cut out a piece of their own heart?[9]

---

[9] This line is 50 per cent me and 50 per cent Aleksandr Solzhenitsyn (although admittedly his is the better half). He was a critic of the conditions of the Russian Gulags and helped to expose them to the wider world. This particularly chopped-up quote is from: Aleksandr Solzhenitsyn, *The Gulag Archipelago, Part I: The Prison Industry* (London, 1974), p.168.

GLOSSARY 1

APPS (APPLICATIONS) This is the main communication method between staff and residents. Residents can't ring up their personal officer, or pop by to see them, so instead communication is done through pink duplicate applications: the resident keeps one copy to prove they sent it, and the other comes to the staff member's pigeonhole. Residents send apps to ask to join the choir, go vegetarian, request to change religion, or to chase up their accommodation plans for when they leave.

CARE AND SEPARATION UNIT (CSU)/SEGREGATION UNIT
More commonly known as the 'seg' or the 'block'. You'd say something like, 'Susie had a fight and now she's down the block.' If you watch American prison dramas, the CSU is what they call the SHU or

'solitary', but over there they use it more as a punishment – solitary confinement. In our prison it was more to isolate a problem. So you're put in there for small stretches of time when you've been fighting or are suspected to be carrying drugs. You would never get marooned down there for a year like you do in *Orange Is the New Black*, though, and before you start imagining a Miss Trunchbull-type chokey arrangement, it's just like a normal wing, except with only a couple of pads. It can be a bit lonely down there but effective as a way to stop drugs or drama spreading.

CANTEEN The canteen is a large sealed plastic bag of shopping that comes on Monday afternoons each week. It's ordered on a canteen sheet the previous week from a catalogue of products including toiletries, tobacco (before it was banned across all UK prisons in 2018), biscuits, noodles and coffee. Because a week's pay only usually covered one pouch of tobacco, everyone would be desperate for their packs on Monday and would often feign illness in my workshops if the canteen trolley was seen through the window making its way up the corridor.

CLOSED/OPEN PRISON In men's prisons, residents are separated into categories from A to D based on risk and the severity of the crime. Depending on their sentence, they'd be housed in the relevant-category prison in their area. Closed/open is the female alternative. Because only 5 per cent of prisoners in the UK are female, there aren't enough prisons to categorise people geographically *and* by severity of crime, so everyone goes in together. Instead, those who are closer to release or 'lower risk' might be transferred to an 'open prison'. These tend to be 'free flow', so people can walk between buildings unescorted. Residents can be categorised on different wings depending on the crime or length of sentence, but, in reality, you want to avoid putting co-accused (see below) residents together or residents with a conflict history, so it's a bit more complicated. You end up having the murderers in with the shoplifters, the paedophiles with the parking-fine avoiders. Like one big happy family.

GOVERNOR Governors are essentially prison managers. Each prison is run by a selection of 'governors' who are overseen by the 'number one governor'. In day-to-day conversation, this governor can genuinely just be called 'the number one' – for instance, 'We'd need backing from the number one', 'Can someone radio the number one?' During my time in prison I had two governors and, before the second one arrived, I wasn't even sure what the number one's full name was.

The other governors are what you'd call in a normal workplace 'department managers'. There's a residential governor, a security governor, etc. In what sounds like a secret service parody, the number one becomes the 'Gold Commander' when there's an emergency. The other governors could become 'Silver Commanders'. In an everyday emergency, you get in touch with Oscar One – that's the code for whichever governor is the overall manager for the day, and has the special corresponding radio. Initially, the whole business makes you feel as though you're in MI5.

MOVEMENT A section of the day where residents can move freely between buildings. In a closed prison, no one can move unescorted between buildings except when 'movement' is called. (In an open prison, you can move around within a given area whenever you like, so you can take yourself to appointments or the loo. That's what's known as 'free flow'.)

All residents are counted before movement and after. The count can take a few goes to get right. Until you get it right, it's 'standfast', which means all residents have to stay where they are. No one can get out tools they need for work – needles, scissors, floor-cleaning machines, etc. – until everyone is ticked off. I realise counting sounds like a simple job but it's actually quite easy to get caught up with someone's panic attack and miss calling the numbers in, or to forget someone's in the loo and so give the wrong count. I was responsible for causing a standfast more than once.

Outside movement, anyone moving between buildings must have a patrol officer escorting them, like a human taxi.

PAD This is the word staff and residents use to refer to cells. It also doubles up as a widely used prefix – for example, a cell search is a 'pad-spin'. You share your room with a 'pad-mate'. Your pad-mate is who you've been 'padded up with'.

PRISON ESTATE The prison estate is just a way of referring to the whole establishment. You might talk about the 'stability of the prison estate' or say that the 'whole estate is on lockdown'. I hadn't thought to define it until a friend commented that it was an odd use of the word 'estate'. As though the prison was a group of council houses or the home of landed gentry.

RESIDENTS The collective term used for people in prison. It was changed from 'prisoners' in 2017 after we came under a new governor, but this language shift is also a general change working its way across the system. I often hear people outside of the prison service talk about 'offenders', 'inmates' or 'convicts' when they want to refer to people in prison. Aside from sounding like something out of *Porridge*, those terms aren't universally accurate. Most prisons also hold people who are awaiting trial, so technically neither 'convicted' yet, nor proven 'offenders'.

WING A collection of cells. All prisons are split into 'wings' – the one I worked in had eight. Each had its own character and personality. There was the detox and induction wing, the enhanced (privileged) wing, the 'basic wing' for people with reduced privileges, etc. We had a long-term and serious crimes wing, which made us a 'high-security' prison. Years before I was there, it used to be called something like 'the dangerous and psychotic prisoners' wing', but was allegedly renamed 'Acorn' in a bid to reduce the stigma.

HUSKIES NOT BUSCIES

If you've been in a community centre or school in any small town in the UK then you will not have to exercise your imagination much to picture the inside of our classroom. Speckled commercial carpet enclosed by walls of display boards, bordered by strips of brightly coloured corrugated cardboard waves. Laminated instructions on how to walk safely with a pair of scissors are Blu-Tacked next to an alarm bell. Alarm bells are distinguished from light switches by a thick yellow border, although when fumbling for a switch in the dark the two are still easily confused. Long tube lights which glare fluorescently run in lines down the ceiling, one set flickering irritatingly at half-hour intervals. A ubiquitous safety notice above the sink reminds users that the hot taps are, in fact, hot.

Aside from the alarm bell, it is only distinct from its secondary-school equivalent because of the metal detectors and large iron gates that close around its outside entrance, and because of the shadow boards where numbered scissors, Stanley blades and needles hang on hooks against matching black silhouettes painted onto the back of the twice-locked cabinet. The cabinet keys are signed in and out to staff daily.

I was there to help run an inclusion project, a gateway into education or employment for those whose mental health, behaviour or disabilities meant they could not join mainstream education or go into prison employment in the kitchens, gardens or sewing shop like most women in prison do. We were a haven for the socially anxious, emotionally bottled-up, post-traumatic, and those with attention deficit disorder or new to prison. We were also often a home for those who were difficult to place elsewhere for whatever reason: the lady with a Zimmer frame; the woman who liked to believe she was a cat; timid foreign nationals who we could only communicate with through mime.

Our courses ranged from self-expression in papier-mâché to exploring identity in calligraphy. From making plans for the future in creative writing, to recording storybook readings to be sent home to children who were in the care of assorted relatives or foster homes. The general aim was to create a space where people could decompress some of the swirl of emotions and experiences they arrived with. Mostly we asked people how they were doing and invited them to respond in paint and pen.

Our classroom hung off a long corridor, which ran for half the length of the prison grounds and was aptly named the 'main corridor'. Its doors led to five wings, two treatment rooms, the segregation unit, three association rooms, a drug treatment space, the 'through-the-gate' release team (who set up housing, college courses and welfare claims in preparation for people to leave), the dining hall and our department: creative industries.

We shared the area with the sewing sisters and the British Institute of Cleaning Science (BICS) training group which taught commercial cleaning. The latter buffed and shined the lino floor of the main corridor each morning and afternoon so that course attendees could complete the hours of practice necessary to qualify as commercial cleaners. Because of the heightened probability that a BICS qualification could lead to a job on release (as opposed to our qualification in soft-skills and art), the BICS course was always very full. Sometimes the floor was cleaned several times over the course of a morning to make sure that everyone progressed to the next module. (The main corridor was immaculate and recognisable by its stinging hospital scent of bleach.)

In the early days of my job, before a new governor had brought with her dashes of colour, the place was, however, resolutely grey. Grey breeze block walls and grey display cabinets lined the grey pathway. Gates split the corridor into long rectangular sections. The gates were once white but as they were opened and shut hundreds, and then thousands, of times, the white paint had begun to chip off to reveal the dark grey Teesside steel from which they were made.

The display boards broke up the grey ever so slightly. They advertised drug treatment courses, programmes for victims of domestic violence, tips on mindfulness, Open University courses, chapel groups, coping mechanisms and whichever themed week or day was next in the calendar: Christmas, International Women's Day, a Macmillan fundraiser, Olympics week and Diversity Day. Like a Tokyo pedestrian crossing, the corridor bustled and buzzed during movement, collective voices bouncing off the non-porous walls and floors. And then the voices split up and were carried out, as the corridor all but emptied when activities segments began. A pattern which would repeat at each movement as people ebbed and flowed around the estate.

Within the grey walls, however, the activities departments, the healthcare centre and the wings held a hive of colour and activity. In our classroom we had new people starting every three weeks and joining the cohort, and others who, after a few courses, had progressed to employment, which meant the dynamic, as well as the curriculum, constantly evolved.

*

The most popular, but my least favourite, of our regular courses was 'Card Mania!'. It was a three-week micro-enterprise challenge in which the group was split in two and each half had to start a temporary *Apprentice*-style business designing greetings cards. The best ones were chosen by wing-based market research, scanned onto an A4 'catalogue', and posted in the window of the wing office, along with a stack of 'apps' which the residents used to order the cards. The second half of the course was then spent making the orders and sending them out. Over the last week, my colleague Alice and I would become postwomen; delivering everyone's cards through their door-flaps and dealing with angry complaint apps when the heart was stuck on wonky or someone got delivered the wrong one and demanded to be allowed to 'take it back'. On week four, we would receive a stack of apps that didn't make it in time, and then Alice and I would spend our lunch break as involuntary craft entrepreneurs, fixing the previous week's dud cards so Lois had something to send to little Robbie for his birthday. We were suckers for that kind of request and everyone knew it.

The first week, though, was spent learning the techniques: collage, quilling, iris folding, origami, tea-bag folding and embossing. Unless you're over 65 and part of a fairly tedious village craft group, you've probably only heard of a few of these. They are the preserve of those who have a large amount of free time and whose main communication is through letters. An unlikely alliance between prison enterprise projects and local craft groups keeps these techniques from extinction.

But everyone loved the course and we were always oversubscribed for it. And, yes, it obviously prompts innovation and teamwork – and spending mornings meticulously making personalised cards for loved ones and friends' loved ones is a good use of time. So I swallowed my secret desire to ruin a perfectly good course with repeated attempts to introduce everyone to Grayson Perry or Kate Tempest, or to get everyone to reflect on the inaccurate representation of prisons by the tabloids by making their own alternatives.

To numb the tedium of technique week, Alice introduced a 'pun day'. We would come up with a stack of puns and everyone had to pick one and make a corresponding card. You got to choose from such (witty) gems as: 'You've got a pizza my heart', 'Squid Goals', 'We make a good pear', 'Have an egg-cellent day', and, in what I thought was the cleverest thing I'd ever come up with, 'Huskies Not Buscies', a local spin on the more well-known 'Pugs Not Drugs' catchphrase.

'Buscies' were big news in the prison and as much a part of the local vernacular as any of the three-letter acronyms that peppered our training pamphlets. It's the slang term for the medicine Buscopan. *Buscopan*, I hear you ask, *isn't that for IBS?* Correct. It's a humble muscle relaxant – prescribed to soothe stomach cramps. A common-or-garden, over-the-counter drug, available at all good chemists. And it had been wreaking havoc in the prison for weeks.

At first you only heard about it here and there, accompanied by disbelief (who's smoking what?), but as it was passed from resident to resident, healthcare gradually stopped prescribing it and before long we were dealing with several incidents a day. It first made its way into prisons as part of a heroin withdrawal pack given out to new arrivals to treat the cramps that come with the first few weeks of withdrawal on the detox wing. You'd also get painkillers, a methadone prescription (your 'script') and colouring worksheets – the prison had jumped on the mindfulness bandwagon and was dishing out patterned colouring sheets and acupuncture magnets to everyone, from addicts and trauma victims to stressed staff. (While this sounds like a sarcastic review of the mindfulness programme, I actually used both methods and can happily recommend either, especially after a difficult morning.)

The Buscopan epidemic was pretty desperate, but it was also a classic example of resourcefulness and entrepreneurship. It's said to have started when some risk-happy withdrawer at a male prison decided to skip the instructions to 'swallow one tablet three times daily' and to smoke it instead, along with everything else in the pack, to see what would get him high and help him check out of his headspace for a while. While the aspirin was a failed experiment, Buscopan, it transpired, worked a treat. So he sent a letter to his girlfriend telling her the good news, and from there word travelled fast.

By 'worked a treat' I mean that on some people, and in combination with certain antidepressants, it gives you a 'gouch'. This is when your brain traffic is interrupted by a cloud of happy mist and your head lolls about your chest like an old man trying not to nod off in an armchair. It numbs you – 'a downer', rather than 'an upper' like you'd get from cocaine or LSD. I gather that it's like taking a holiday from your own brain. (Note that gouch is pronounced g-ow-ch rather than goo-ch. A goo-ch is the bit of skin below a man's anus.)

Unfortunately, in combination with other medication, or using other makes of the same drug, or really for no discernible reason, it can also leave you hallucinating that the hot water boiler is the shower, cause you to brush your teeth with the dustpan, lick the floors, or sign away your canteen to your opportunistic cellmate. These are all real examples. In other depressingly real examples, it led to irreversible psychosis. Some Busca-fans, known locally as buscy-crumbs or the less glamorous 'shit-tablet junkies', have been observed biting officers, experiencing incontinence to the point of wearing nappies, and habitually banging their heads against the wall. Rumour has it that one user was transferred by six officers to a psychiatric unit after Buscopan-induced psychosis left her in a hallucinatory state where she tore off her clothes and masturbated in front of staff.

But on the plus side it's 15p a tablet from Asda and, at the time, not technically illegal. Until the law caught up with this over-the-counter-innovation, it carried the same weight in court as smuggling in a cervix full of paracetamol. This meant it was a behavioural offence rather than a criminal one. You could lose your TV for having it, or spend time in the seg, but you couldn't get extra time on your sentence or extra offences on your record. It's changed now – on a recent visit, one woman I spoke to got 14 extra days inside for 'endangering others through passive inhalation', but these things take a while to plod through the system and, as it turned out, you could smoke a lot of drugs in the intervening period. It's easy to be judgemental – and, particularly after a lack of sleep, I can be an expert – but anyone who's so keen to numb their own thoughts and feelings that they'd risk not ever being able to come back from that probably doesn't need our help in the criticism department.

As an aside, Fererro – the makers of the Kinder chocolate range – may be pleased to know that Buscopan, as with other drugs, is often brought into the prison via Kinder Eggs – or, rather, the little plastic capsule that contains the toy. Some residents could fit four or five in their internal storage compartment (vagina), which is a lot of tablets. With so-called 'revolving door prisoners' going in and out regularly on short sentences, people could put in orders, like sending someone out for milk.

The prison value of these was £5–10 a tablet, depending on the current level of supply. In other words, you got a fantastic return on your 15p Asda investment, with not too much risk. A good business proposal. And if you ever need a resourceful and entrepreneurial person, you are spoilt for choice in prison.

Without the policy backing to penalise Buscopan users, the prison had their hands tied. They increased bang-up on culprit wings, and installed large fans in the corridors to blow away the candy-floss-smelling smoke so staff didn't pass out and have to go off sick. The Buscopan crisis was both heartbreaking and a pain in the arse (try teaching watercolour painting to someone intermittently passing out).

But to return to the aforementioned card – by lunchtime, the team that shotgunned 'Huskies Not Buscies' had produced a small, square design featuring a husky outlined in glitter, accompanied by the copperplate anti-drugs advice. Our market research confirmed the card's popularity, as did the department's officers who were all given copies by the team.

Caitlin was in charge of the production logistics. She was a bit of a 'prison mama' – smiley and tattooed. The sort who gathers up the younger girls, makes sure they've done their washing and advises them against biro-ink prison tattoos and abusive boyfriends. Women like Caitlin were a dream to have on the card course because they would weed out the wonky cards and make sure we were meeting orders, while I doled out the tools, fielded pastoral crises and translated step-by-step instructions in mime to anyone who struggled with English. Without the Caitlins of the group, card production went down the drain the moment we were confronted by an interruption, which would end up with me and Alice making cards on our lunch break again.

Word of the husky card spread and the officers trooping in and out of the room to have a look prompted a visit from Rory, the hospitality teacher. Rory had slick hair and designer stubble and had been talking about leaving the post to start a hipster coffee shop for as long as I'd known him. His hospitality module was on pause while they trained a second teacher, so he'd been moved to cover the dreaded 'induction course'. Induction, which explained the prison's systems and helped you to set goals for your sentence, was compulsory and therefore full of disgruntled attendees who had done it at the start of their 13 previous sentences and made their dislike known. I'd have wanted to quit too if I was on induction. Rory was quite harassed.

'You won't get that husky through,' he warned. 'It's not appropriate, what with the current climate. Who came up with it?'

'I can't remember,' I lied.

'Well, I'm surprised you let it go in.'

I thanked Rory kindly for his advice but assured him that it had gone down well with the other residents and the department's officers, and that no security department would be so uptight as to ban an anti-drugs message.

In fact, aside from Rory's concerns, the card received such rave reviews that Caitlin anticipated large orders and got the group to up production so that we were prepared for the stack of apps which would arrive a few days later.

Pulling the catalogue together to display the card options was another matter. The prison had an ancient scanner, but the Windows 2000 preservation club which masqueraded as the prison IT network had never managed to connect to it on my account. Collating the catalogue involved spending half a morning traipsing round to find someone whose account could successfully make the link. It was a task, I often reflected, that would have taken under five minutes had I been able to bring in a phone, photograph the cards and send them through to my email. But alas, phones that are brought into prisons wreak such havoc that it is a criminal offence for staff to carry them – a fact that is frequently reiterated – and an action of such severity that I'd rather have spent a day sketching the card designs into the catalogue by hand with my mindfulness colouring pencil than risk the wrath of Her Majesty's Prison Service.

(The Queen, incidentally, is not particularly popular in the prison system. Due to everything being branded with HMP – Her Majesty's Prison – she gets a lot of unwarranted flak for cancelled visits or boring lunch menus. 'I don't know how she gets to sleep, that fucking Queen. Swanning about in a palace while she's stuck me in here in a double with some scruffy cunt who doesn't change her sheets.' Although I don't feel particularly strongly about the monarchy, I felt a little sorry for Elizabeth about the whole misunderstanding.)

The next morning we continued production. By mid-morning I'd received a note asking if I could please visit the residential governor after my morning session.

'It'll be that card,' Alice remarked.

'The card is fine. It's anti-drugs! What's wrong with people?'

I knew it was the card, though. I went to visit the Activities office *before* posting up the catalogues in case I had to make a return journey to take them down.

As usual it had been left to Yasmin, head of learning and skills, to break the news. She had a kind manner and long pink polka-dot nails. The sort of colleague who was nice and so often given more work than her counter-parts. She was, in equal measure, lovely and worn out. She ran an after-hours group helping people study for degrees while they were in prison, and she immediately endeared herself to me because she always came to see our exhibitions of the residents' artwork.

She looked apologetic, holding one of our prototypes between her cheerfully manicured fingers. 'I'm sorry, but the residential governor's had a look at this Buscy card you're making and it's a no. Don't get me wrong, I like it myself and I don't doubt it would be popular, but the concern is that it would be for the wrong reasons. They think it makes light of our recent crisis, and adds to the cult status of the drug. You'll have to take them out of the catalogue.'

Sigh. 'What about the ones we've already made?'

'Don't make any more, but I guess there's no harm in letting people take home their prototypes.' She folded the card she had in front of her and sadly tucked it out of sight in the top drawer of her desk.

Funnily enough, it was the second time Alice and I had got into trouble over the card course. The previ-ous year, one team had decided to brand their business 'Criminal Cards', written in alternating pink and black block capitals. Those catalogues were removed from the office walls and returned to our desk with the Blu Tack still on each corner. They had an accompanying note from our seniors saying, 'As some of our residents are on remand, and therefore have not been proven guilty, the term "criminal" is both inaccurate and inappropriate.'

When I got back to the classroom Alice was sitting at the desk with the stack of catalogues. She had already begun cutting off the bottom-right corner to remove the offending card.

'It was the husky, wasn't it?' she said.

I unlocked another pair of scissors from the tools cabinet and took half the pile.

I told the group the next morning.

'Fucking ridiculous,' Caitlin commented as she redrew her card-orders tally sheet.

The 25 we'd already made were divided up and went back to the wings with our group to be stuck on pinboards or sent to friends. And of course, the good businesswomen that they were, I'm sure no one missed the opportunity to trade them for coffee and fags, especially when the unofficial market value of the 'limited edition' card shot up after the ban. You can't say they learnt nothing on the enterprise course.

EIGHT THINGS TO KNOW ABOUT KEYS

1. You should keep them hidden when not in use – don't hold them in your hand between gates; they must be kept in a pocket or your leather key belt instead. In the unlikely event that one of the residents has a photographic memory, they could remember the shape and make a replica key.
2. All gates and doors must be 'proved' after locking – i.e. given a good rattle back and forth to make sure they are properly locked. Also a good way of taking out frustration if you've spent the morning trawling through the hoover bag because someone has dropped a needle and you need to find it before everyone's allowed to leave (for example).
3. Always lock the door behind you before you unlock the one in front.

4. If a staff member asks you to leave the gate open for them, they must be within a few metres of you. Otherwise you are kindly asked to ignore their request. The only exception to this rule is if officers are running towards a riot bell.

5. If a lock will not shut, or your key breaks in the lock, wait by the gate until someone finds you – nothing you have to get to is more important than the security of that gate. Do not, under any circumstances, leave the open gate unattended.

6. If you find an unattended open gate, you must first lock it and then report it to security. The culprit can then be discovered using CCTV footage and be re-trained on proper use of gates and keys. The dread of repeating the key training provides sufficient motivation to keep up the locking and proving.

7. Never try to leave the establishment with gate keys. A loud alarm will go off and you will look like a moron.

8. Any resident caught trying to grab keys off staff will be assumed to have intentions of escape and be required to wear a brightly coloured 'escape suit', so they are more easy to spot. Ours were a fetching orange but rarely worn. In the YOI (Young Offender Institution), though, disgruntled teenagers in neon onesies were a brilliantly common sight.

SHE WEARS A PAPER CROWN

With the absence of blood relatives (although there were a handful of these inside), it was quite normal for residents to arrange themselves into temporary families. Intimate relationships, sisterly connections and, most commonly, older women who took younger women under their wing. Friendships that outlasted the end of prison sentences.

Nicki was one of these women who collected maternal characters and became their surrogate daughter. She had been imprisoned as a teenager for being involved in a Manchester gang and had grown into her adult body inside the locked gates of G wing, under the care of older women who became one collaborative parent. It was a mutually beneficial relationship: they still happily advised the now 33-year-old Nicki about how best to separate her washing, as though they, too, in flexing their maternal muscles, were filling an invisible hole. It was her mix of honesty and creativity which made her easy to like. She lacked the bravado that was the defensive mantle of many other residents and was quick to ask for help.

Although older now, she was like an insect trapped in steel-barred amber: her time inside had served to preserve the adolescence that she'd arrived with. Her teenage style – choppy pink hair, eyebrow piercings and cartoon t-shirts – had been frozen in time, along with the symmetrical rows of deliberate scars which lined her right arm to signal her membership of the gang that had landed her in here. She sang the mid-noughties pop music that had been the soundtrack of her years before, and was always asking me to google who Britney was now dating, or explain what Facebook was like so that she felt up to date.

Nicki joined us for my first art course looking at identity. We'd started the course by constructing a series of collages on A3 card, made from ripped newspapers, glitter, photos, coloured card, felt tips and buttons, to represent the past and future version of our lives. (We'd have to flick through the newspapers before bringing them in in case we unwittingly handed out news related to one of our class members and had to spend the rest of the lesson policing the gossip.)

The left-hand side of the A3 sheets represented the

past. Each time we ran the activity this side was filled with pictures of parents and cats alongside pencil-drawn syringes, photographs of houses entitled 'the children's home', vodka bottles and stick-figure portraits of those who had steered the path in the wrong direction and, it was decided, were best left behind.

In contrast, the right-hand side usually featured Laura Ashley sofas Pritt-sticked next to adverts for garden furniture, wedding rings, champagne glasses and pictures of smiling children. Nicki painted a pop trio that she wanted to form on release, herself still drawn as the teenager she had been on arrival rather than the middle-aged woman that she would be when she left the following year.

'Can I take some buttons back to sew on my jumper?' she asked, holding up the jar of assorted buttons that I'd handed out for the exercise. Her behaviour status was the highest of the available levels – enhanced – and so she was allowed certain privileges, including a needle in her pad for mending clothes. It was, however, a little harder to get hold of fabric, embroidery thread and buttons for any more ambitious customising projects.

'Nope, definitely not,' I replied. We were on a tight classroom budget and stuck rigidly to the rule that materials were not allowed to be siphoned off to the wings.

'I knew you'd say that,' she replied, giggling. 'What about our collages? Can we take our collages back?'

'Yes, you can keep all your work, just not materials,' I told her.

'And if my collage was made of buttons and thread. . .?' She winked and raised her eyebrows.

'Your collage can be whatever you like,' I replied, pushing the box of threads to her across the table. 'As long as you can explain how it relates to you,' I added, raising my eyebrows back in warning.

'It *is* about me! It's a random selection of buttons artistically arranged! And I'm random and artistic.' She continued, 'The buttons and thread are the border anyway – the bit in the middle with the band is about me.' She proceeded to sew the 20 buttons she'd selected around the border of the pale yellow card, humming as she stitched. Her good mood was infectious and, before long, she'd persuaded everyone in the class that their posters really ought to have a few buttons too. I loved moments like that, when, despite whatever was going on in the prison, you forgot momentarily where you were. Things might be bleak but, fuck it, we were going to laugh at buttons, and we were going to crochet our hearts out. After Nicki had sewn her neat border she turned to help Susan, a lady next to her who was in her sixties with prematurely arthritic fingers.

'I could never do anything as nice as yours,' Susan sighed, running her fingers over Nicki's neat card.

'Yours is brilliant,' Nicki replied, pointing to the collage. 'It's just missing a few buttons.'

Nicki began sewing little clusters into each corner of Susan's poster. 'They can be friendship buttons,' she announced. 'Now you have a little of me on the collage about you. Do you want to add something to mine?'

Susan eventually conceded a pair of heart-shaped stickers placed on the back of Nicki's poster. 'I didn't want to ruin your lovely design,' she explained.

I was not under any misconceptions that Nicki was all sweetness and light. She had dark, silent days and flashes of anger that clashed with the cheerfulness and coloured buttons quite unexpectedly. A week later, she painted a self-portrait on the theme 'My home is my body'. We'd encouraged everyone to paint the best version of themselves, and her almost violent piece was in stark contrast to the contributions the rest of the class produced. It interrupted an A3 line of women in ballgowns surrounded by pets and families with its painted black background. The picture stretched from one corner of the paper to the opposite one and showed a naked body with legs and arms tied together. The body's veins were visible through translucent skin, its face almost completely taken up by a wide-open screaming mouth. Underneath in pencil the painting's title was written: 'Home doesn't exist'. Absence of home wasn't a story unique to Nicki, but to see her painted naked and restrained in

declamation of it was quite shocking. Like a car crash –
so awful but you can't look away.

'That's a bit much,' one of the officers commented
when he came to check that everyone had left my
room.

And it probably was. It would never make the education department newsletter but its addition at least
made for a more representative collection of pictures. I
placed it next to a picture of a holiday abroad: a beach
scene with a wide umbrella and seaside horizon.

Nicki rolled onto the next course, where the focus
moved from self-reflection to making Christmas cards.
During the first week I taught the group card-making
techniques. Once each day's techniques had been mas-
tered, the class would design their own cards incorporating what they had learnt. Nicki fashioned a card
which would double up as a wearable crown, with a
greeting written inside the hat's circumference. She
was so taken by these cards that she made one every
day for the practice week, incorporating each new
technique into the card's design – origami, folding,
collage and so on. So each day the cards increased in
flamboyance – felt tips replaced by sequins and feathers,
more stitched buttons and glitter edging on elaborately
folded paper.

'What's the carry on with the hats?' one of the

movement officers asked as he saw Nicki queuing up to leave the classroom.

'Oh, she's just wearing a card she made – it's a hat-card,' I responded.

'Residents can't wear hats,' he said, shaking his head, 'it makes it hard for them to be identified on the CCTV. One of the wing officers said she came back with one a few days ago as well.'

I doubted very much that Nicki's crown would serve to make her *less* identifiable, but spoke to her nevertheless the following day as she packed up to leave.

'Nicki – could you not wear the crown out of the classroom?'

'It's not a crown. It's a card,' she responded petulantly.

'I know,' I replied, my patience wearing thin after an unproductive morning. 'So put it in an envelope. It's going to stay here with me if you keep leaving wearing sequins.'

'Okay!' she said, and then made a point of elaborately folding the crown into an A5 white envelope. 'Is that all right?'

'Much better,' I replied, ushering her out of the room as the officers began to pat everyone down before they left the classroom.

Once all the residents had gone, I filled out the accompanying behaviour books (in block capitals to avoid my usual scratchy illegible handwriting): 'HILLARY

WAS POLITE TODAY AND CONTRIBUTED TO THE GROUP DISCUSSION. SASHA SHOWED IM-PROVEMENT ON YESTERDAY. NO CONCERNS.' Then I locked away the last of the materials. As I moved a box I saw Nicki had left behind her plastic ID card. New ones cost £5 to buy – half her weekly wages – so I decided to drop it back to Nicki's wing officer before heading off home.

As I walked towards the wing, I could hear laughs and shouts echoing from the building where the wing was based. While the prison's main wings were a deafen-ing cacophony of incessantly rattling gates and shouts, Nicki's separated wing tended to be quieter. I let myself into the wing hesitantly in case I was about to get in the way. I was greeted by Nicki sprinting round the corner, almost knocking into me but instead swerving to fell a yellow plastic sign warning of a wet floor. The shape of a heart had been sewn on the front of her jumper in the cream buttons that she has used to border her poster a few weeks previously. As she ran the buttons clinked and jingled together, the sound of fingers running through a bowl of collected shells.

And, most importantly, on her head was her latest hat-card – which she had clearly just unfolded and crowned herself with. Red and purple feathers hung from its lower perimeter, beginning at one ear and circ-ling her head until they reached the other. The final touch was some googly eyes in the centre of it, staring at me and a pursuing officer. The crown's nine points were painted in alternating purple and red acrylic paint, and in glitter along each point was written the names of those women in the prison who had come to be her family. Queen Elizabeth, eat your heart out.

As Nicki ran along the corridor Susan, whose name was listed on one of the crown's points, shook her head and wagged a warning finger towards her. Nicki grinned and skipped down the corridor in response. The feathers seemed to become part of her hair and, as she spun, they became airborne; she was a craft-box Medusa.

The officer who was chasing her stopped as he got to me, giving up on his half-hearted pursuit, and leant his hands on his upper thighs. 'Welcome to the madhouse!' he said to me, smiling and rolling his eyes.

I introduced myself and said, 'Just dropping back Nicki's ID.' I handed the card over to him. 'She left it in class today.'

'You must be the teacher who keeps sending her back with bloody headgear! They've got more ridiculous every day.'

'It's part of one of our projects,' I explained, grimacing apologetically.

'Yeah, I got that. Good to have her off the wing, though. Getting into something good.' He held out his hand to be shaken, as if he was congratulating me. I felt quite touched and a little taken aback at the gesture. My rather self-indulgent assumption when I'd started had been that the arts and therapy department had the monopoly on compassion, and that we would have to rub alongside the unfeeling disciplinarian security staff. But I was wrong. And I would re-realise this every week until I left. There isn't really a 'pastoral staff' and 'security staff'. Under the circumstances, confronted with someone's pain or progress, everyone became the 'pastoral staff' – teachers, healthcare, security officers and governors. 'Could you put a lid on it now, though?' he asked. 'I'm knee-deep in paperwork as it is without having to run after her, confiscating paper crowns.'

'They're actually cards, it's just that they unfold . . .' I started to explain feebly. 'Okay, I'll keep the crowns from now on.'

I never stopped being amazed by the resourcefulness I saw in prison: paper coronations; temporary families sewn together; jumpers decorated with siphoned classroom materials; rooms redesigned by gated Laurence Llewelyn-Bowens armed with J-cloth curtain tie-backs; misused prescription drugs mimicking the heroin use that was a part of normal life outside; bin-pilfered card offcuts transformed into notice-board designs; Sunday lunches cooked from what could be found on the canteen.

I suspect it's part of being a human, that pull to nest. To construct traditions, relationships, rituals and things around us until our world feels more like ours. A little safer and more familiar. Home sweet home.

MOTHERS

The prison is full of mothers. Mothers of adult children who visit them at weekends bringing their grandchildren in tow; mothers whose motherhood is on pause because their children are being looked after by foster families until they can go back to them and resume their role; mothers whose mothers are doing the mothering for them – an army of grans and nanas collecting children from school and footing bills for food and clothes; and mothers whose children, passed from pillar to post by the care system, had followed in their footsteps and lived just up the corridor on one of the other wings.

There were also, often, mothers-to-be. At any one time there might be one or two residents who had arrived pregnant and swelled larger by the day until they waddled up the corridor, round and full. I always felt that pregnancy somehow seemed to happen more rapidly in prison, as though life was hurtling towards the surface faster than anyone could prepare for its arrival.

Motherhood is revered among the prison's residents in a different way to how it is on the outside. In prison, motherhood is a reduced and long-distance vocation, and so the importance of your maternal role to your identity is even more vivid. I imagine it being similar to nationality. Day to day, being British is an insignificant fact to me; I only notice it if I'm in a different country which doesn't automatically serve milk with tea, or set much store by queuing. Identities have a habit of being most noticeable when you have been removed from the fact. Likewise motherhood, which on the outside is par for the course, inside burns all the more fiercely for its physical absence, and springs out continuously in conversations, carried photos, keenly anticipated visits and deep longing.

These pregnant individuals were therefore treated with great respect and their comfort became a communal matter. Other residents saved them the Penguin bars from their lunch-packs and opened doors for them. If it was thought that they'd not received the proper healthcare treatment, the full wing shared outrage. Staff too treated pregnant residents with greater leeway – they were, after all, carrying someone that was in prison without any charges.

In a way, pregnant residents might be considered lucky. One of the main punishments of prison is that you are separated from your family: at least when you are pregnant your two-person, almost-family remains together, unaffected by the confines of the visiting hall and without requiring the permission from any authority.

Not everyone is separated at birth, though. If your baby is expected during a short sentence, then you can apply for transfer to a mother and baby unit where you can both finish it together. These are more like hostels than prisons. You can't leave them, but you're able to live in a supported environment with your baby. They're tight on places, though, so the authorities have to be convinced you're going to be able to keep the baby permanently after you leave.

In other cases, a family member might collect the baby once it's been born, while the mother heads back to the prison from hospital to resume her sentence. For others who had long sentences and no available family, there was voluntary adoption, or even temporary fostering so the decision could be taken later.

But for those who faced involuntary adoption when their babies were born – where the decision to separate mother and child was made by social services – pregnancy was a time bomb. And if you were in the clasp of addiction, had a long sentence to serve or faced ongoing domestic violence, this wasn't uncommon. For this group, their pregnancy may have been the longest opportunity they'd have to spend with their child during their life.

I had a few pregnant women in my classes but usually they were due out before the end of the pregnancy, so I knew little of what transpired afterwards. Later, there would be Irene, who spent the length of her pregnancy inside the prison but who gave birth a week before she was due to leave, and so interim care was easily found before she could begin the more official proceedings with social services after her release. And there was Zoe, whose baby was collected by an aunt until they could be reunited and begin the same process.

But then there was Paige. I'm not sure if it's hindsight that has increased her presence in my memories, or if she would always have loomed so large in them, but I remember her all the same. She was only in my class for a few weeks. She sewed and talked a little of baby names and about her plan to go to a mother and baby unit for the rest of her two-year sentence but was mostly very quiet. For some, it's immediately obvious that a transfer is not going to happen, but Paige was one of the participants of an in-house skills programme. She was engaging with courses to overcome problems around mental health and addiction and learn coping mechanisms. This meant that her being accepted into a mother and baby unit wasn't as unlikely as it could have been. There was a ray of hope.

After she moved on to a different course, I didn't see much of her, but our little team thought of her often, and wished her well as we saw her plodding her way to the dining hall or to healthcare appointments. 'Not long now!'

Paige's experience was a well-trodden road within the prison system, so I think perhaps the reason she was so often in my thoughts was because it ran in parallel with the first pregnancy I'd experienced. Not mine – pregnant staff are retired to desk jobs – but my cousin Jo's. Her baby was the first one I had noted growing from grape to orange to grapefruit. The first one whose arrival I had anticipated with excitement, and for those final months I was suddenly drawn towards tiny boots and knitted vests in shops in a way I hadn't been before. Jo's hormonal tears were met with cups of tea and outings for cake and back rubs from friends and parents, while I knew Paige's would be coming from behind a cell door. I suspect that's why I kept thinking of her little baby and wondering what size fruit it was too. I wondered whether she'd be allowed to keep the baby. Whether it would be fostered temporarily or adopted. Whether she'd be successful in applying to a unit. I knew that, up until the birth, social workers would continue to pay Paige visits and weigh up that impossibly difficult decision.

Just as on the outside, maternity leave in prison is marked by a pause in employment. (You might also be interested to know there is sick leave and retirement.) So, in the final run-up to the birth, the chapel sent Paige colouring sheets to hopefully help fill the gaps in her day where activity had now been replaced with bittersweet anticipation and antenatal visits. I was optimistic about her chances, but it was grounded more in naivety than accurate expectation. I was still quite green then and had yet to watch a new mother return empty-handed after a birth, but I can tell you there's something gut-wrenchingly heartbreaking about the sight of empty hands against a still-bloated stomach, almost as though it had never happened at all.

I kept my ears open for news of Paige as much as I waited for news of Jo. Paige was first, as expected – and taken to the same hospital as I knew Jo would go to. Then a few days later, she was suddenly back, walking, still bloated, across the courtyard towards her wing.

'She didn't get to keep it,' Sam relayed bluntly. Sam had been in my class at the same time as Paige. We'd all talked about names over embroidery threads. Sam was less surprised than me. She had seen it before. 'It happened with Erica last year too. She got a few days with him because they need your milk to wean him off the methadone, and then they sent her back with something to dry up the milk that kept coming.'

That complicated miracle of new life.

It was the exact opposite, I thought, of everything I'd known about how a baby should arrive. Everything. I couldn't help but imagine Paige in her cell. Milk collecting and drying up on cotton pads and her hands, which might have held a scaled-down human, holding her own curled-up knees or a hand-rolled cigarette instead. It was as though there had been a death, and although I had no right to feel the sadness as my own, it stayed with me anyway. I wondered whether I should ask her about the baby when I saw her next. Whether she would like to be asked if she'd had a boy and what name she'd chosen, or whether it would cause her pain to remember the details.

A day later, as the staff pressed thumbs against fingerprint scanners to collect our keys at the prison gate, we were met by an A4 'death in custody' notice taped onto the notice board, telling us that Paige had died.

It was the worst day I can remember. Crying residents collected in the corridor on the way to activities. The officers, who usually moved people on quickly to their placements, let everyone linger a little longer. The chapel was a strange mix of sombre and frantic as the staff digested the news and supported the residents who'd been most affected by Paige's death, hosting pastoral visits and planning a memorial. Back in class, we made flower-covered tributes to be Blu-Tacked to the door of Paige's cell where her body, still full of birth hormones, had been found.

I thought of Paige again recently when I was with Jo and her gorgeous, happy little boy, Hector. She held her wriggling two-year-old while I helped him to put on the miniature velvet waistcoat my mother-in-law had made him to wear at my wedding. Jo cooed over him in his mustard-yellow jacket with the Thomas the Tank Engine buttons and smothered him with kisses and compliments about what a wonderful page boy he'd be, and how sure she was that he could throw rose petals better than anyone else.

I hope that Paige's child knows that he was just as loved, too.

I MISS . . .

[Gathered from various conversations]

X Travelling on a bus and seeing things go past the window.

X Drinking wine, or, actually, drinking anything from a proper glass that isn't plastic.

X Sex [with a man].

X Sitting on the sofa wearing pyjamas. [You can't wear sleep attire in the common rooms.]

X Having a private conversation on the phone without anyone waiting to use it or getting worried you'll run out of minutes.

X Being able to go and watch all the new films that they play adverts for on the TV rather than waiting till they come out on TV.

X KFC.

X Playing the piano.

X Listening to new music that is not on the radio.

X Listening to your *own* music on an iPod or phone so you aren't forced to listen to whoever on the wing puts their music on loudest.

X Drugs.

X Trees.

X Chatting to old people on benches. [There are very few old people in prison.]

X Having a door you can lock yourself where no one else has the key.

X Silence. [Even at night alarms are tested, there are keys jangling, pipes banging or people shouting.]

X The bakery at Tesco with jam pastries.

X Having dinner at normal dinner time rather than having to eat at half-five.

X Going for a walk to clear your head

X Sunday lunch with Mam.

X Going into a shop and trying on clothes, just to see what the styles look like, even if you don't buy them.

X Drinking Coke from a can.

X Being able to hug my daughter for as long as I want.

X Privacy.

GLOSSARY 2

ACCT (ASSESSMENT, CARE IN CUSTODY AND TEAMWORK)

A file that follows the resident round if they're in a low mood and at risk of self-harm or suicide. Staff observe the resident, ask how they are and write down observations about their mood. They're regularly assessed to review the number of observations (obs) per hour needed. The highest watch you can be on is four obs per hour, through the day and night. These check-ups will take place randomly through the hour to stop the person on watch calculating a time window to make a suicide attempt. Staff are meticulous about carrying out these procedures because if one is missed or rushed because you're busy and something happens on your watch, I'm told the guilt makes it something you'll never forget. If this happens you also have to appear in coroner's court.

IEP (INCENTIVES AND EARNED PRIVILEGES) STATUS The IEP system is the star chart equivalent of the prison system: you can be graded up or down depending on your behaviour and each level comes with privileges or sanctions. The basic theory is that good behaviour leads to more benefits. You can be:

BASIC The lowest IEP status. It's the punishment level, so you might get wages or TV docked.

ENTRY Entry level is what you're on when you arrive, unless you've been transferred from another prison and carry your status with you.

STANDARD Average IEP status. After a couple of weeks on entry level your behaviour is reviewed and if you've done nothing to result in a different banding, you'll likely get put on standard.

ENHANCED The highest IEP status. You can up your chances of being 'enhanced' by taking on a mentoring job or becoming a wing rep (see below) to prove yourself. The enhancement perks vary from prison to prison, but in ours you could have a cross-stitch needle and were able to buy things from the Avon catalogue. You're also generally more trusted, which has its own rewards.

MULTI-FAITH ROOM The room inside the chapel which is used by non-Christian groups – basically anyone who doesn't need the altar in the main chapel. Our group was quite informal, so we often used it too. We shared it with Muslims, Buddhists, Pagans and Jehovah's Witnesses. If your stated religion doesn't have a chaplain currently working in the prison then you can request one in. Everyone is entitled to one hour of worship a week in their chosen religion. People weren't supposed to pick'n'mix and go to a few different ones because it went over their entitlement, but in reality some people just loved chapel groups and so we turned a blind eye to the fact that they were coming to everyone's groups and requesting crystals, rosaries and Qur'ans.

NOTICE BOARD Every pad has a notice board. As you're not technically allowed to decorate walls and wardrobe doors, these provide a canvas for residents to customise their room. There were some spectacular notice boards constructed from received cards, family photos and pilfered card scraps. Some were colour-coordinated to match homemade curtain tie-backs, and others were changed and renewed with the seasons, like a spring clean.

PRIVATE CASH This is money that's been put into a resident's prison account from outside by friends and family. You're allowed a £10–25 'drop down' from this private cash as spending money each week depending on your IEP status. If you call home most days, then your weekly phone bill can be more than £25. The prison phone, for some reason, is vastly expensive. There are solutions to this in the pipeline – Skype calls and a voicemail system – but unfortunately they haven't reached us yet. If you don't have private cash, then you pay for your toiletries/food/phone credit on prison wages. It's sort of like pocket money if you've done your weekly chores and attended education. When I worked there, you'd get £10.50 a week for full-time employment, unless it was in the kitchens, waste disposal or sewing sisters, which got you a bit more. If you're on basic (see above) your daily pay is cut until you're upgraded again.

RESTRICTED STATUS If you're 'restricted status' then your escape has been deemed to cause a significant risk to the public. This means that you'll be housed in a designated 'secure' area and you're probably high profile. At our prison it meant that they were buddied with an officer whenever they left the wing. It also meant that no photos of them existed. Even on their files and ID cards, there was just a silhouette.

(Rumour has it that's to prevent anyone selling the photos to the press for a tidy sum.)

TRAINEES This is the word they used instead of 'residents' at the Young Offender Institution I worked at. As they were all under 18, they were legally required to be in some sort of training or education just like on the outside, so it was a pretty accurate description.

WING REP The resident who represents the wing to the staff at regular wing meetings and makes requests on behalf of the other residents. It gets a slightly bad reputation for being a somewhat Mickey Mouse process. One resident had been trying to get pineapple added to the canteen catalogue for six months before she decided the process was fruitless (pardon the pun) and resigned.

CODE BLUE

The radios for each department are signed out from the gate each morning. They spend the day attached to the belts of their corresponding officers, blaring out in crackling voices what's going on around the estate.

Incident in the dining hall.

Permission to move residents from creative industries back to the wing.

Code red.

All staff during their training week are provided with a selection of codes. The idea being that in an emergency you can communicate what's going on through the very public prison radio system without having to be as vivid as 'someone's just cut their wrists in B wing bathroom', which might spread general panic. Instead, this is 'code red'. 'Code blue' is respiratory. In prisons where there are heavy Spice problems causing people to go into comas, the 'code blue' call punctuates the day's radio dialogue quite regularly, eliciting groans from officers before they peg it up the corridor to help.

(I was told on several occasions that there was also a 'code brown' for if someone's had a crap in the wrong place or smeared it on the wall, but it was never called so I did not establish whether this was a real thing or just a very situation-specific running joke.)

Your department also has a code so people know which one you're calling from – something catchy like echo-five, or M2GG.

If there's been an emergency – if, for example, someone's phoned from the outside to report a family death, or someone's climbed on the dining-hall roof – you have to radio 'Oscar One'. That's the radio that will be held by the duty governor. They're the kingpin of the communications system and will inform other departments that need to know what's arisen.

Because there are no mobile phones in prison, only office landlines, you also use the radio system to find out where anyone is – a bit like an elaborate game of hide-and-seek. 'What's the nearest extension for Officer Duckworth?' the radio asks, and everyone looks around to see if they can locate her. Then the person nearest her replies, essentially, 'I've got her, and she's agreed to now go and stand by the following landline waiting for your call.' It made me think of that challenge Greg James did on Radio 1 where he hid somewhere around the UK and members of the public had to call in if they saw him until someone found out he was near a Pizza Express in Liverpool.

I was too low down in the pecking order to carry a radio. You got one per department and ours was held by the sewing sisters instructor.

(This, I realise, might seem like a rather inconsequential summary of an internal communications system, but I hope it will give a little context to the story that follows – the only time I was called upon to remember a code.)

It was the start of a new course. At the beginning of any course you never knew which residents might have been allocated to you for the next three weeks. There was a list, of course, but as we got a lot of new residents, many of the names were unfamiliar and did not provide much clue as to what the following three weeks would be like. There were always a few carry-overs – people who had been on the previous course and wanted to stay on. This time it was a woman called Christine. She had said very little on the previous course. When she had spoken, her answers were short and surly and she'd participated to the minimum amount required. I was therefore surprised that she'd put her name down for the next course, both circling and highlighting the option on her job preference form at the end of the last course.

It was one of our usual courses, the rather cleverly named 'A Stitch in Time'. Clever because it was both a sewing course, and its theme was about time: 'learning from the past – dreaming for the future'. The course sometimes felt a little contrived but often it turned out that this was the first time anyone had asked these women what their dreams for the future might be, and so we continued on the theme.

I set out our introductory paperwork, wrote my name on the board and counted the needles to be sure that we had the number listed on our weekly tools check before we started. The group filed in over the next ten minutes, waiting to see who else was in the class before they committed to a seat.

Sally came in first. She had been in the class on a previous sentence the year before and, despite her unflattering reputation, I was very fond of her. She had a short back and sides, homemade tattoos and wrists ribboned with self-inflicted scars. She always wore men's clothes, and was particularly proud of an oversized Adidas t-shirt worn over tracksuit bottoms. The triple-stripe design on her outside leg ran into the one on her t-shirt, making it look as though someone had drawn Tipp-Ex lines down the length of her. Sally was unpopular among staff because she could come across as rude, but I thought she was not unlike my mum in her communication. My wonderful mother is eccentric and simply does not see the need for polite formalities, calling them 'fluffy bunny talk'. She will announce at a party, 'I've stopped having fun now. I'm going to go,' much to the surprise of the host. The only difference is context, and the level of profanity employed. My mum is a middle-class artist who lives on the outskirts of London, and so her blunt delivery is chalked up to artistic temperament rather than insubordination.

'Miiiiiiim's Island!' Sally shouted at top volume as she came into the classroom. 'We're going to have a nice old time in here, aren't we?' She ran up and put her arm over my shoulder.

Sally had always called me Mim's Island. She had mis-remembered the name of the kids' film *Nim's Island* and I didn't have the heart to tell her she'd got it wrong. Even when Sally was not in the class, I had been met with the familiar greeting every day at 8am, accompanied by a knock on the office door as she passed it on the way to collect her morning medication.

'Fuck sake,' she began as she read the description on the board. 'I'm not doing any fucking sewing then. It's going to be a sleeping week for me.' She mocked falling asleep on the desk. She said this each time but I knew from previous courses that it was a nervous front and that she would produce something brilliant by the end of it.

We were joined next by neatly turned-out Amy who had, within minutes, taken photos of her three children out of her pockets to show the rest of the class. 'Fucking lovely little family you've got there,' Sally commented.

Several nervous new arrivals followed, recently transferred from the induction wing (where you are placed when you first arrive), and a couple of chattering friends who moved chairs around so they could sit together.

Next arrived our class mentor, Kate. Because she was the class mentor, Kate came on every course. Her job was to make sure the glitters stayed in the right colour pots, sort the paper into correct-size piles, and give one-to-one help to anyone who needed it. On the previous course we'd had someone whose sight was so poor that Kate had practically completed her whole project for her, audio-describing the process and putting the almost-blind lady's ideas into designs she would never properly see. Kate wore jeans and colourful tops rather than tracksuit bottoms and had her hair cropped into a bob.

She was the mentor because she was endlessly kind and patient, spending hours with the most demanding learners and helping us to clear out old cupboards over her association time. But her kindness was often taken as weakness and she found it difficult to say no. I suspect it was this fact that led to a crack addiction, visible now through lost teeth and shiny scarred-over burns along the sides of her fingers. Kate's art projects were often given away, along with her tobacco from her canteen, to whoever asked. I knew people were putting pressure on her to return the art cupboard supplies back to the wing so, despite her dedication to the job, we watched her carefully. We did not want to lose her, which would be the inevitable conclusion if she were caught on the wing with any classroom supplies.

Last came Christine, accompanied by another lady dressed in a tracksuit not unlike Sally's. 'We've got to sit together,' Christine said gruffly, prompting one of the new arrivals to swap to an opposite seat so that there was space to accommodate this request. As soon as they sat down, Christine swung her arm around the back of her girlfriend's blue padded plastic chair. This is the kind of thing that in the main education block would have been disallowed, but in our bridge project we picked our battles. I could have insisted on their separation but, undoubtedly, it would have led to conflict, official warning, and eventually a sacking. (In order to mirror external employment guidelines, all work placements in prison have a rule that three written warnings lead to a sacking.) This pattern was why they were in my class in the first place, and I reasoned that there was little point in creating an enemy of this new learner before I knew anything about her.

Christine introduced her girlfriend as Lilly. I had actually heard of Lilly and, to be honest, my heart had sunk a little when I saw her name on my list. She had been sacked and passed on to different departments with a predictable regularity – for refusing to work, kicking off at staff and faking sickness.

She was, like me, attention-deficit, but in contrast to the therapy course and coping strategies I'd been given growing up, she was not uncommonly dependent on a number of medications to stabilise her mood. The NHS and prison budgets, it seemed, could stretch to pills but more rarely to counselling or CBT.

Lilly put her cards on the table early on, during the 'any questions?' round of the course introduction. 'Let's be honest, miss. [I began courses by explaining that I should be called Mim, but, without fail, was called 'miss' for at least the first week by anyone new.] I'm here because my girlfriend is on the course. Do I have to actually sew?' She put her feet up on a chair after she spoke as though to demonstrate that this was less a question, and more a statement.

Christine had recently been moved on to a different wing away from Lilly and it seemed that our project was the only place they could be together. Lilly made it quite clear she'd rather be in the kitchens but had sacrificed her dignity by agreeing to sew patchwork squares in order to have some quality time with her beloved. I could see already it was going to be a tiring arrangement.

The dynamic was not helped by the first day's task of 'life mapping', where each participant was asked to draw a map; a timeline of the places and people that had made up their life's journey so far.

'Am I supposed to draw a load of fucking children's homes, then? And stick figures standing outside for all the blokes that abused us?'

I could see her point.

'No, not if you don't want to. Just go back as far as you feel comfortable,' I replied, now thinking it had perhaps been the wrong activity to start with.

Lilly drew felt-tip-coloured circles and grey handcuffs and, in case there was any doubt, labelled them in biro capitals 'DRUGS' and 'JAIL' before setting her pens back down and returning to chat to Christine, holding her hand under the table. Christine, in response, added a pink heart underneath Lilly's pencil-lead grey handcuffs on which she wrote, 'Christine loves Lilly'. At least, in this small way, the story-map had a nice ending.

The rest of the group were still working on their maps. Sally, who refused to draw, was leafing through old newspapers from the collage cupboard, trying to find words in the headlines that fit her life story – which she could then cut out and stick on. Her design was taking a particularly long time because she kept getting distracted, reading out stories from 2011 about some-one's murdered lover, and ranting about the injustice of it all.

'We're going to the loo,' Christine announced, her and Lilly both getting up.

'Wait,' I said. 'One at a time to the loo. It's in the class contract.'

'Fuck off! Really?' Lilly responded. 'Alice never made us do that.'

Alice, the other creative industries tutor, had had Lilly a few months earlier for a short course. The toilet rule wasn't new; we'd just been a bit lax on it until a depart-ment crackdown on toilet smoking a few weeks earlier led to a tightening up.

'Really,' I replied to Lilly. 'Otherwise we'll have every-one in the loo sharing a fag and I'll get a bollocking from the sewing sisters.'

'Send me back to the wing, then,' Lilly retorted. 'This is a fucking joke.' Except in the case of visible illness I could not send people back to the wing without listing it as a work-warning on their file, so I was reluctant to do it.

'Lilly, I'm not going to fire you, I'm afraid, because that's us both giving up and I think you're better than that.' It was probably an equal mix of stubbornness and optimism, but we did not easily sack people from the course and prided ourselves on being the department that held onto people against all odds, people who struggled and kicked but often then grew to love the group and grow within it.

'I wish I was still in Alice's class,' Lilly said pointedly, but then returned to her seat and doodled a biro border around the life map.

As Lilly was leaving at the end of the long morning, I tried to say something encouraging. Her reaction was not uncommon and our team found that moving past a few blips was well worth it if it meant we could keep someone long enough to get to know them. 'Thanks for staying, Lilly. I know it's hard to continue in the class when you're pissed off, so I appreciate you've stuck it out today. It's meant that I haven't had to put anything on your file, which is what we both want.'

'Thanks, miss,' she said, looking at the floor before speeding up to join Christine in the search queue to be patted down before they left.

We continued in much the same vein during the first week. She'd hold Christine's hand and issue statements designed to shock at random intervals: 'I'm a slut, me', 'I can't wait to get out and take loads of drugs', 'good job they took my kids away – I'd only fuck 'em up'. But she stayed, always leaving the classroom loudly proclaiming, 'Bye, then, won't see you tomorrow, I'll be sacked by then.'

At the end of the first week, I sneaked a look over

her shoulder at her self-set goals sheet, which we asked everyone to fill out at the beginning of each module. She had written in the left column, 'Stay in a job for a whole week' and next to it she'd drawn a tick in green felt pen. Underneath the sheet lay a self-portrait she'd completed during the week, a face split down the middle showing two halves of herself. One with dark graphite circles ringing the eyes and a collaged syringe; the other half with watercoloured rosy cheeks and bright blue eyes.

Seeing me looking she turned over her goals sheet and used the self-portrait to cover it. 'You've done amazing,' I told her, taking the self-set goals sheet back out so I could sign it off. I rang through to allocations to let them know that I'd be happy to continue having her in the group.

The next week, Lilly began to talk; not just the shouted remarks – although we had plenty of those still – but little snippets too of why she felt that the world was so against her. And, she was right, it had been. It made sense that she had that angry, defensive voice, spitting back at the world in reply.

By the third week we'd moved on to a group piece, constructing individual felt squares to be sewn together into a patchwork quilt made up of their future dreams. It was mainly populated with designs of symmetrical, Edwardian-looking, four-window detached properties with red front doors. Assembled, they made a white-collar hamlet with matching front gardens of red and yellow flowers. This design was, in part, because our materials order was delayed and so our two remaining colours of felt – red and yellow – featured heavily in all the designs, and partly because the biscuit-cutter dream of a home and an intact family was all that most residents ever wanted. I never saw dollar signs, mansions, or holidays in Ibiza – or the living-on-a-barge design that I would have made. It was mostly just neat houses, with lockable front doors. The exercise never failed to make me realise how utterly and completely lucky I was.

Sally, next to Lilly, had constructed an image of a syringe onto her bottle-green felt. She decided that she'd discovered a quicker and easier solution to sewing and had used PVA glue instead to attach the pieces of the syringe onto the felt. She had conceded to some sewing, though, and the word 'NO' was embroidered in capital letters above and below the syringe in yellow embroidery silk.

'It'd just be a lie if I did one like that,' Lilly said, turning Sally's template for the syringe over and over in her fingers. 'The first thing I'll do when I leave here will be to go and score some gear and just check out of my head.'

'Do you really want that, though, Lilly? Even though it's taken so much away from you?' I asked.

'It's not taken anything away,' she replied, 'because I didn't have anything in the first place, and if I come off the drugs, I'm not suddenly going to get back this lovely fucking life I've never had. I'll just be left with the memories I was trying to block out in the first place.'

It was a sentiment I heard over and over again – although not one that you'd ever find portrayed in the paintings, quilts and collages that were chosen by the education department to be hung on its walls. Instead, we considered it progress to see patchwork lines of abandoned bottles and crossed-through heroin foils across the bottom edge of a quilt, soothed by the simplicity of it all. As though life *does* magically come to resemble an Edwardian hamlet once you've given up drugs and alcohol. But, of course, Lilly was right. The drugs were rarely the main problem; it was what had happened before.

She did in the end sew a house with two stick figures waving out of the windows, partly because a pro-drugs message might have ruined the group's opportunity to have the piece put into an external exhibition had it been rejected by Acceptable Activities (who were responsible for assessing whether your project was allowed to go ahead and whether it was okay to leave the prison), and partly because Christine was nudging her to return the gesture of her own felt square which pictured them holding hands under a sun.

At the end of the session, Lilly stayed behind while the others lined up in the search queue so I could chase up an app for her that she'd written about an appointment with the mental health team.

'You know, Mim, I used to think you were a dickhead, but I like you now. Not as much as Alice, but it's all right in here,' she said.

In spite of myself, I couldn't help smiling as I walked the ACCT documents back to the wings to rejoin their owners. Not as good as Alice, but at least I wasn't a dickhead. It felt like a victory.

During the last week of the course we held a miniature exhibition where the artists wrote paragraphs on lined paper about what inspired their artwork, and we invited the surrounding work parties to come and see the finished pieces laid out on the Formica desks, their maker standing nearby to watch the onlookers' reactions. One of the braver residents would read out a summary of the course to give the attendees a little context, and occasionally the head of learning or allocations popped down for a look too.

'I'll do it.' Lilly volunteered loudly to read the summary. 'It's not that fucking hard.'

We had laid out the exhibition but were waiting for the sewing sisters to return from their slot in the library before we declared the exhibition open.

Lilly began practising the introduction we had written together. 'Over the past three weeks, we've been using textiles and sewing to explore the people we are, and the people we want to be . . .' She read it without looking up from the page so as not to get distracted by the rest of the class.

I sat on a desk, watching, and reflected on our three weeks just passed. I felt unbelievably blessed to be allowed to see these courageously shared parts of people's lives: the best parts and the worst. Lilly finished her paragraph and gestured for Sally to introduce her piece.

And then it happened all at once. Lilly fell sideways off the chair she had just sat down on and began convulsing on the floor. For that first split second I was immobilised by the surprise of it, the violence of the shakes, her eyes rolled back into her head. Then the adrenaline kicked in.

Christine had rushed to the floor. 'Christine, make sure that you don't let her bang her head,' I said. 'I'm going to get hold of healthcare.' She held Lilly's head in her lap to prevent it hitting against the side of the table where she fell, while I racked my brains to remember my training. It was blue. Code blue. I ran into the sewing sister classroom to use their radio – but they were still in the library along with the radio. The corridor outside and the surrounding rooms, usually filled by the hum of floor-polishing machines, the shouts of BICS students and teachers and the tinny echo of radio communication, were oddly, and unhelpfully, quiet. I tried the office phone, hoping to get through to the central board, but it wasn't picked up and, while it rang and rang, Lilly fitted back and forth across the floor.

I unlocked the door to the main corridor and pulled in a passing officer. 'Blue. It's a code blue,' I said, gesturing to the fitting Lilly who was being held by Christine, who had pooled the jumpers of the rest of the class and was laying them over her.

The officer spoke down the radio and the main corridor suddenly became a flurry of activity – healthcare staff and officers sprinting towards the incident to provide assistance. Two healthcare nurses knelt down next to Lilly.

'Good job protecting her head,' they told Christine, who continued to kneel there.

I stepped back, relieved that the healthcare professionals were now there to make everything all right. The prison-staff sprint that followed any riot bell or radio code was a reassuring sight, and I was glad of their calm, reassuring voices.

Then the nurse called me over.

'Do you know her well?' she asked, nodding her head at Lilly.

'Er, I guess so,' I responded.

'Well, you start talking to her while I do her observations. Just ask how she's feeling.'

I felt rather honoured as I knelt down on the carpet where she still lay, curled up. 'Lilly,' I began. She'd stopped fitting by this point so I held her hand. She looked towards me as she began to gain consciousness. 'It's Mim here. Can you tell me how you're feeling?'

'Earghhh, I feel . . .' she trailed off and laid her head back down.

'Take your time, Lilly. Just tell me when you're ready.' I hoped that I sounded more confident than I looked.

She made eye contact with me and then answered in a muffled voice, 'Like I've had an orgasm, miss.'

'What was that?' asked the nurse, who hadn't quite heard.

'Er, like an orgasm, I think she said,' I replied, unsure of whether it was a medically relevant fact. The officers standing around failed to conceal their smirks.

Lilly continued, gaining momentum and strength as she did, 'You know, miss,' she insisted, 'like when your legs go all shaky and jelly-like after you've come?'

'Mmm,' I replied, non-committal.

Christine, Sally and the staff and class members broke into laughter which pierced the tension and Lilly began, with Christine's help, to slowly sit up.

'Well it is!' she said defensively. 'What else am I going to say?' And then, taking in the scene of the gathered officers and the blanket we'd constructed from collected jumpers and jackets, she began to laugh herself.

Courage, Brené Brown says, starts with letting ourselves be seen. It is telling the story of your whole self with its flaws and bad experiences and imperfections.[10] And each time we let ourselves be seen and it ends badly or we face rejection, the more courage it takes to repeat the process the next time. Lilly stayed on for the next course, and the next, and continued to teach me and the other learners that sometimes strength looks and sounds like vulnerability.

---

[10] Brené Brown, 'The Power of Vulnerability', https://www. ted.com/talks/brene_brown_on_vulnerability#t-1009564 (date accessed: 15/10/18).

SHE CAMPED OUTSIDE
THE GATE

It was easy to forget you were in prison when you were in the chapel. The lino floor and Brillo commercial carpet tiles that covered the rest of the prison graduated into a proper carpet as you crossed the threshold into the wide space. Because it lacked the lino it was also without the bleach smell that hung in the air on the main corridor. Instead, it was replaced with either tangy incense if the Catholics or Buddhists had just met, instant coffee if there had been a group meeting or, if you came in the afternoon, the slightly less appealing salty-stale smell of whoever's lunch had just been microwaved.

The chapel day featured a jumble of intensely profound moments, daily pastoral admin and the regular business of people practising their different faiths. Weekly mass, faith support groups, Bible and Qur'an

studies, prayer group, drug rehabilitation days, medi-
tation and yoga classes, memorial services and pastoral
cups of tea. The teas were my favourite. Moments when
you could absent yourself from the hubbub of the prison
and sit in the multi-faith room chatting over steaming-
hot tea served in the chaplaincy's special supply of
ceramic mugs. Regulation prison mugs are made of a
thin blue plastic and the ceramic upgrade was a luxury
afforded on these pastoral visits.

It was on one of these appointments that I sat with
Catherine to talk about her release.

We began by making coffee in the chapel's kitchen-
ette. Catherine pouring hot water over coffee granules
and powdered creamer and stirring the mixture until it
turned a caramel colour. My mug was borrowed from
Father Jack, the Catholic chaplain. Across its side it had
a captioned cartoon about cardinals which I didn't get.

We'd planned to talk about Catherine's transition
back outside, put some support in place, pray, and to
make arrangements to meet at the gate so I could drive
her wherever she needed to go. We were the only organisation within the prison system that was allowed to
work with people while they were in prison and also ac-
company them through the gate and into their life after.
Back then, most staff were discouraged from even stopping in the street to say hello to women they'd worked
with inside, in case contact outside the prison led to

pressure to bring items back in. I understand the logic but the policy did exacerbate the feeling that to leave the prison was to fall off the end of the conveyor belt of support, cut suddenly from the people and programmes these women had been working with on the inside.

We'd had a busy year so Catherine's drop-off was the first one I'd done for a while. She sat down and ran her fingers up and down the coarse pale blue fabric that covered the padded chairs, occasionally picking at a loose blue thread on one corner. Catherine was 19 and usually the life and soul of our classroom and chapel group. She would tear up the wing afterwards, showering the pads with glitter pocketed from the classroom by way of a blessing. She spoke about her son on every visit to the chapel and carried pictures of him with her, folded in her pocket, ready to be shown to staff and other residents.

But today her thoughts were not forthcoming. 'Can I light a candle?' she asked, gesturing towards the low table in the room's corner which held a stone cross and a handful of small blue tealights.

As with everything you wanted to do in prison, usually you had to put in an app if you wanted to come over to the chapel and light a candle. It was then added to the day's timetable, just like visits or haircuts, with people on the list being sent over to the chapel at morning movement. You'd know who was coming because in the large chapel diary, every day under the heading

LAC (light a candle), were one or two names, listed next to the reason why. It was often for children's birthdays or for an anniversary of a death. Some days, when a relative had died and the resident couldn't make it to the funeral, we held a small replica service to mark the day and remember the dead. On those days, we also thought about those mourners on the outside who were gathering in black, with somebody else missing who shouldn't have been.

The residents who came to the chapel group often seemed soothed by the ritual, and so our cups of tea were interspersed with candles lit and blown out in remembrance and hope regardless of which faith they were assigned to or whether they'd booked an LAC. Although it's not my tradition, I still find myself stopping at cathedrals and churches to light candles and offer prayers for those women who shared something of themselves over those flickering flames and special ceramic cups.

We made our way over to kneel in front of the low table of tealights. I passed Catherine a match and secured the rest back in their locked drawer, bringing with me the laminated card that held the liturgy we used.

'Who would you like to light a candle for today?' I asked.

'Is it all right if we light one for me?' she replied tentatively.

'Of course it is. Is there anything in particular you'd like to pray about?'

'I don't want to go,' she said quietly, looking into her lap.

I was, by this time, quite used to hearing people say this, but each time that fear of freedom, coupled with the idea that the best life we could give a person was to be locked on a wing, was equally heartbreaking.

'Of course you do. We've been thinking about this day for months,' I replied gently.

'I don't. I'm so scared. Here is the safest place for me. I've got food and somewhere to sleep and people to help. What have I got out there? No house, no family, no support, nothing. You don't know what might happen to me,' she said, blinking away the tears that had settled in the corners of her eyes.

She was right. I didn't. But I could well remember the state she had arrived in earlier that year. One side of her face black, blue and raw. Stitches, administered by the healthcare team on arrival, held together a deep cut which protruded from her hairline. She had glazed eyes from too many pills and under her sleeves were dark imprints – small circular bruises that ran in a line across her wrists. When asked what had happened, she just shook her head, unable to relive the memories.

As the weeks went by, and she got used to the protection that the prison's locked gates afforded her from those who would prey on her vulnerabilities outside, she stepped out of her silence. And with healed scars, stitches removed, and the support of the makeshift family she constructed for herself among the wing's other residents and the prison's staff, she relaxed. Although there were flashes of her experience in moments of silence and worry, she became an integral member of our little chapel group.

'You've not been told anything about your housing?' I asked. I used to be surprised by this, but the regularity with which our team chased up housing requests meant that the shock I had once felt in realising that women were released into doorways and community day centres was now replaced by disappointment, and even resignation.

'I've put three apps in asking about it but no one is getting back to me,' she said.

I sighed. 'Do you want me to call your offender supervisor and chase it up?' Everyone had an offender supervisor, who would oversee their sentence and was their go-to contact for this sort of thing.

She nodded, although it was more a symbolic gesture of support on my part than anything else. We both knew that, even if I managed to get a reply from her officer, with five days to go, it was likely she would join the six out of ten women released from prison to no address, who would therefore likely be back with us within the cycle of our classroom's curriculum. She lit the match on the spare empty box we kept by the candle display and, as she passed the dancing flame from match to candle, prayed aloud, 'God, please protect me and don't let anything bad happen to me, keep me safe, and look after the girls here too.'

She gripped my hand tightly, as though the pressure with which she held on was a physical prayer, as if the force with which she was hoping would, in itself, keep her from harm.

'I'm going to try and come back in,' she announced as we washed up our mugs. 'I'll do whatever it takes. Not hurt anyone, just get caught shoplifting or something. I'm not going to last five minutes out there, I just know it. It'll go wrong again and then I'll self-destruct. I'll end up drinking again if I'm on the streets on my own.'

We dried the mugs in silence and stacked them back on their trays. I felt more useless than I ever had, offering painting and prayers but not a lockable front door.

'I'm sorry, Catherine,' I said as the patrol officer unlocked the chapel doors to escort her back to the wing. 'I'll let you know what they say about your housing and I'll be outside the gate from eight-thirty, so whenever you're released, just come and meet me in the family centre. We'll get a McDonald's breakfast, then I'll take you to wherever you need to go.'

She laughed weakly as the patrol officer led her away. 'Maybe I'll even have somewhere to go by then.'

'This is ridiculous,' I ranted to the chaplaincy team. I felt at the end of my rope with the whole place and so we'd headed out for lunch in the Tesco canteen up the road. 'We're sending her out like a lamb to the slaughter. Honestly, what do they think is going to happen? That she's going to sleep in a doorway like a sitting duck with almost zero support and somehow stay away from the people and the drugs that landed her in here? I know exactly what's going to happen and what she'll end up doing for a bed, and so does she. No wonder she's so fucking terrified.'

'It's such a shame – we're one of the wealthiest countries in the world!' Sylvie, the Muslim chaplain said, shaking her head. 'It reminds me of that woman a few years ago, who camped outside the gate.' I looked at her nonplussed. 'It was probably before you started. She got released, then had her first meeting with probation in the visitors' centre just outside and then she just sat down in the car park on one of the grass verges and stayed there. We'd thought she'd gone a few days later, but then, at the end of the day there she was, sitting on the same verge alternating between there and the bus shelter bench. I can't remember how long it was, a good while, though. There was an email that went round telling us not to sit and talk to her. I think they thought she might get us to pass messages in or something. She just didn't have anywhere better to go. I wonder what happened to her.'

'That is terrible! I can't believe that wasn't in the papers,' I replied, mopping up the last of my gravy with a remaining chip.

'Yes, because the *Sun* is really going to bother coming out over a homeless ex-addict ex-offender. It doesn't exactly read well as a headline.'

As predicted, my call to Catherine's offender supervisor revealed that, while they were doing their best and had something in the pipeline, there wasn't any supported accommodation free. They were still waiting for the bed to become available, so it wouldn't be ready until a few weeks after her release.

What was the point? I thought, clearing old drinks cups and crisp packets out of my glove box in the prison car park while I killed time before Catherine's release. Where exactly would I even drive her? The car journey was more for the company than for any practical reason. I guess in ferrying her from one unsuitable place to another we at least played out the idea that being released looked like progress.

She was released at 9.30 and completed her first appointment with probation in the purpose-built block just outside the gate. (Having the first appointment immediately outside the gate meant that those released back into sofa-surfing in crack houses would at least definitely make it to the initial meeting.)

Catherine put her white bin bag of possessions into my boot, a pair of red trainers visible as they pressed against the side of the thin plastic. We drove towards the McDonald's on the other side of town. I'd expected her to be fascinated by the changes that had happened in a town she hadn't seen for almost a year. I pointed out the new cinema being built and a finished park renovation which sported large black and gold gates, but she leant her face against the window and absent-mindedly chewed an already bitten fingernail as though she hadn't noticed how the town had looked before.

We arrived just in time for the breakfast menu and ordered a McMuffin meal and vanilla latte for her and an egg and cheese bagel and Americano for me.

'It'll be all right,' she said. ''Course it will. I'm a fighter. I've always had to fight for myself and I'm stronger than I look.' She delivered the line in a persuading voice, as though she was talking herself into believing it. 'I spoke to my cousin last night who gave me an address I can stay at, and then after a bit I can get myself sorted. Get a place of my own. I was thinking I could get a frame for the picture I did in creative industries and put it up on the wall. I've still got it. I put it in a book to keep it straight. When the flat's nice and I've got myself sorted I can start supervised visits with John.'

She smiled at the idea and sipped at her vanilla latte. 'I'd forgotten how good these were!' she exclaimed, scraping the foam that coated the sides of the paper cup with a wooden stirrer.

Getting back into the car I typed the address she had written on a scrap of lined paper into my satnav. The route took us 20 minutes away into a suburb where we wound around the neat roads of a housing estate following the screen's blue arrow, until we came to the cul-de-sac where Catherine was to stay and counted along to number 6.

The front garden was high with weeds through which protruded the plastic legs of disused garden furniture lying on its back. Heavy bass filtered out through the front door, which was ajar.

'Whose house is this, Catherine?' I said, realising that it was the first time I'd asked.

'I don't know,' she said, her knuckles white as she gripped her other hand, but she forced a smile.

'I'll walk you in,' I said.

'No,' she replied. 'I think you should stay in the car.'

I'll admit that I was grateful not to be shown into the house, aware that what I found inside would probably not help me to sleep any easier that night. Some weeks later I would visit another woman and find her front door kicked in and her house overtaken with bodies slumped on sofas. A man didn't stop injecting himself even as I asked who he was and why he was in her house. She was hiding upstairs, arm tied above the elbow, and a needle on the floor next to her. 'I'm sorry, I'm so, so sorry,' she said. 'They came in, selling gear and now they've robbed me. I can't get them to leave. I never wanted you to see me like this.'

I turned to hug Catherine. 'If you need help, just call. You can reverse the charges. Or if you can't get to a phone then go into the Salvation Army kitchen. They know me and can tell me how you're doing.' I handed her our 'moving on' letter. It contained a list of contact numbers accompanied by 'good luck' notes from the chaplaincy team. We said the Lord's Prayer together in the front seat of the car and then I watched her walk through the front gate and into the house.

I saw her a week later at a community meal I help to run. 'Catherine! It's so good to see you. Are you okay?'

Her eyes were glazed and she swayed slightly as she spoke.

'It is what it is,' she said, smiling under tired eyes.

'Is your house sorted yet or are you still staying at where I dropped you?'

'No,' she paused. 'Not there. It wasn't too good there. Bad things happened,' she said, not inviting any further questions. 'I'm sleeping in town.' She threw an arm towards the open window.

A man in his fifties interrupted, putting a hand on Catherine's shoulder. 'Now, what are you saying to my girlfriend?' he said, addressing me.

'Leave it, Chris, I know her,' she replied. I knew Chris too, as it happened, so did all the other volunteers, and the police. He smiled and left us to go outside for a smoke.

'He won't leave me alone,' she said, shuddering. 'I was in a doorway last night but he says I can sleep at his tonight, until I find somewhere better to go. I think I'm going to. He's nice enough and I'll just be awake all night in town otherwise. You can't close your eyes when you sleep out there.'

'Catherine, please don't go back to Chris's,' I pleaded.

'Why? It's the devil you know or the devil you don't. And nothing worse can happen than already has,' she replied.

'What's happened to the housing they were sorting out for you? I thought you could go into it this week?' I asked.

'I met the housing lady yesterday and she said they could put me in that bed on the same day, as long as I hadn't drunk alcohol or used drugs in the last week, and I told her I had so she gave the bed away to someone else. I'd be in there if I'd lied, but you know me, I'm not going to lie. But what did they expect? I've been on the streets. I needed something to take the edge off.' She stumbled and I found her a chair.

'Are you on the list for a house somewhere else? I could take you to the housing drop-in tomorrow?'

'It's not worth it. I'll be back in soon. I'm doing everything I can to go back inside.'

Frustratingly, it sounded like a fairly sound strategy. The safety of the gated prison was far preferable to the uncertainty.

'It's funny,' she continued, 'when you don't want to get caught shoplifting, they follow you around the shop and jump on you the moment you pocket a pack of gum, but when you want to get caught, you can't get arrested for love nor money. I've been walking out with bigger and bigger things that I don't even want. Just walking right past the security guard, looking them in the eye. But they're just not noticing me!' I couldn't help but laugh at that, imagining her striding out of Tesco with a large inflatable ride-on crocodile which was, after the plan failed, given to the children who played on benches in the town's square.

Chris returned. 'Coming back to mine then?' he said to Catherine.

'Thanks for offering, Chris, but I've found somewhere else for her,' I said.

'Yes,' Catherine replied, shooting me a grateful look,

'thanks but I've got somewhere else. Maybe next time.'

I hoped my card had enough money on it to cover the Travelodge bill. It was more to soothe my conscience than anything, I reflected, booking her into the hotel. Because one night really wasn't going to make much of a difference. She'd make her way into town the following morning and begin the cycle once again. And tomorrow I would not be there with my middle-class guilt and my credit card and, no doubt, Chris's offer would be. Cynically, I was just insuring myself against hearing some bad news the following morning, which I would struggle to digest knowing that I could have prevented it.

Catherine disappeared for a while after that, but I was passed irregular updates about her wellbeing most weeks through a chain of people.

'I saw Catherine today,' Gareth, who ran the soup kitchen, would say. 'She says to tell you she's okay and not to worry.'

Or a call from a support organisation: 'We have a woman called Catherine McStay who said you could give a character reference for her?'

Surprisingly, though, these third-hand messages never came, as I expected, from the prison staff – despite Catherine's efforts, she was not back inside.

And, eventually, a message from a guest at the soup kitchen let me know that she had been placed in a refuge.

There is a stage, it seems, when things can become so bad that you are bumped up the housing priority list.

A fortnight after the move, I called the hostel to see if I could visit.

'She slept for the first two days solid,' the complex needs worker told me, 'but she's been around more now. She's been weeding the garden today and then has a drug and alcohol appointment. She came on a trial period because we were a bit nervous to take her with her drug history but she's been clean since she arrived.

'I guess she just needed someone to take a chance on her.'

VETTING YOUNG OFFENDERS

[The scene opens into a classroom in the otherwise deserted education department of a young offender institution. Two teachers – Mim, keen but fairly clueless, and Matt, an actual rapper – are sitting at a desk with recording equipment, headphones and piles of paper. Mim has been seconded to the young offenders' rap workshop on the basis that she writes poetry and can help Matt with the recently introduced progress-measurement paperwork she already uses at another prison. They are listening to radio programmes recorded that afternoon by the trainees in the class and filling out the content-assessment sheets required before they can be aired on National Prison Radio (NPR).]

Mim: Okay, we've got 46 minutes and 36 seconds of recording time to go through and vet.

Matt: Do you want to split it in half and do all the checks on your section, or would you rather we both listen to it all and I'll fill out the violence and inappropriate attitudes section of the form and you can do drug references, victim awareness and illegal activity?

Mim: I reckon split it in half to save on time. If we find something that's on the banned list, do we need to edit the reference out? I'm not sure I'd know how to do that.

Matt: Nah, the radio staff will do that. We've just got to time-stamp the references and then it's up to them if they want to cut it.

[Both teachers begin listening. Time passes]

Mim: Do 'tits' and 'fine ass' come under inappropriate attitudes?

Matt: Err, they play Akon on NPR so I think they're okay with those. Stamp it anyway I reckon? I don't think you can over-stamp.

[More time passes]

Mim: Okay, I think I've got one. If in the rap it says they're in the gallery with a Pen Ten – is that like a shooting gallery, with a gun?

Matt: [Laughing] Let me listen to the lyric.

[Mim rewinds the track and replays the lyric]

Track: *I'm in the gallery, hitting up a peng ten* . . .

Matt: Nooool Not a gun-gallery, a gallery in a club; they're just saying they've seen a girl who's so peng, she's a ten! Do you want me to check over your half?

Mim: Oh yes, definitely.

SMUGGLING VEGETABLES

A box of tomato seedlings are sitting in a line of matching square black pots on the low table in the education staffroom. Written on a scrap of cardboard was a note: 'Free to Good Homes'. It was rather an odd interruption to the usual staffroom offerings of Madeira cake and chocolate fingers.

'Where have these come from?' I asked, picking up a couple of medium-size plants to be taken back to my patio.

'From the gardens,' the on-duty officer replied, as he made break-time tea. 'It's more hassle than it's worth taking them, though – you'll have to get a gate pass from security. The gardens used to do beautiful veg boxes – corn, courgettes, tomatoes. But no one bothers taking them now since security have cracked down on it.'

'Cracked down on vegetables?' I replied, incredulous.

'Why? In case we sell them to crime obsessives on eBay as limited-edition prison produce?'

'It's about things going out of the premises. It's data protection. You know, making sure no one's taking anyone's data out.' He shrugged.

This was making less and less sense. 'Taking data out how? Written on the leaves of a lettuce?'

He shrugged again. 'You ought to see what they've got in there, though. The size of those leeks!'

He went to leave the staffroom, opening the door with his elbow as he was holding a cup of tea in each hand, and calling to me to lock the door after him.

The gardens for the prison ran along two sides of the education block – not far away from the main residential, induction and healthcare blocks that made up the rest of the prison. They were the lesser-used sides of the education block, however, away from the main entrance and walkway, so unless you were looking for the vegetable patches you were unlikely to stumble across them. It was also rare for staff to visit other departments without reason, so after six months in the job, I had never been to the gardens. I had learnt, from the confused questions I'd received when found pottering about the industrial-scale kitchens and dining room one lunchtime to see what they looked like, that the prison – as well as being legally private – is also culturally discreet. It was important that everyone knew where you were lest you be taken hostage, and people were wary that confidential conversations might be overheard by unrelated people. To wander into another department out of curiosity was not banned, but definitely not the done thing.

But I had long thought that being part of the ten-person gardening team was the best job in the jail. Not only did you get to look after the main gardens, but you were tasked with planting borders, flower beds and hanging baskets throughout the prison. So, although most of the staff had never visited the actual gardens department, its presence was known by its satellite projects which peppered the estate. Pansies filled the courtyard where new residents were brought in, the exterior of the healthcare block was planted with neat dahlia rows, and alongside pathways were manicured lawns and anemone borders. Those boxed-in explosions of flora provided an antidote to the distinct lack of green space inside the prison, and every guest I took in, to give a talk or demo a new Christmas craft, was taken aback by its villagey verges. Had the prison been able to enter the Britain in Bloom competition, I have no doubt it would have been placed.

After my teatime conversation with the lovely education officer, I decided to embark on one of my lunchtime explorations. I knew only vaguely where the gardens were, so spent the last 20 minutes of lunch treading the circumference of the education block to find its entrance, getting in via a vehicle gate. As I wrestled the heavy door bolt back into place, a voice came from the nearby building. 'There's a normal gate the other side. That's so we can get the mowers and tool truck in and out.' The voice came from a man in his fifties who was sitting cleaning a gardening fork in the entrance to the small brick building which held the tools and machines. 'Everything all right?' he asked in a tone which indicated he was wondering why I had come.

'Yes, good thanks. I've just come to see the vegetables. I'm told you have some very big leeks?' I replied.

His face brightened as he put down the gardening fork and came towards me. 'Some of the biggest in the county!' he exclaimed. 'I've been a leek grower for years – used to win the regional prize at the Leek Show. But it got too political, you know? The same families winning every year, seedlings going missing, accusations.' He continued to relay this snapshot into the world of competitive vegetable growing as he led me along the path, past a patch of onions and into the first of a series of polytunnels, introducing himself as Robert. The place was notable for its smells and sounds, but only because they weren't the ones we were used to. The usual strong aroma of prison bleach tablets which made the buildings smell like a hospital, and the constant trill of metal on metal as gates were locked and proved were conspicuously absent here among the rows of vegetables. It sounded and smelt like normal life.

'There she is!' he said eventually, pushing aside some polythene sheeting.

What greeted me was not, at first, recognisable as a leek. My grandma is herself a leek grower, but her veg patch yields leeks, at best, about the size of an arm. Instead, these vegetables, whose green leaves fountained up from the top and spilt over on the soil, were, at a conservative estimate, the circumference of my thigh and protruded exactly vertically from the soil bed for the best part of a metre.

'Oh my word,' I exclaimed, gobsmacked. 'You grew that?'

'Not me, the women on the gardening course. I teach them how to grow giant veg. We've got big carrots too, and onions, tomatoes, peppers. The lot.'

Robert took me on a tour around the remainder of the garden, picking ripe tomatoes to try as we walked through the polytunnel aisles where bulging produce was trying to escape into the path from both sides.

'Where does it all go?' I asked.

Robert sucked air in through his teeth and shook his head. 'We used to sell it at the gate. A box for a pound for the staff to take home – but no one's going to bother queueing up at security over their lunch break for a few onions. It's been a pain with the gate passes.'

I nodded. I had, myself, returned the two pots of tomato seedlings to the staffroom table after the officer's comment rather than bring such a trivial matter to our overstretched security department.

Robert continued, 'Kitchens don't want it because they've already ordered in what they need and the women aren't allowed to buy it on the canteen, so I'm afraid most of this lot gets composted.' He gestured to a large wooden compost bin at the side of the plot.

For the first time since I began my job at the prison, I felt I had discovered a scandal. An entire work party were growing magnificent veg which could feed 20 families, and a load of it was going to decompose back to soil. Although it was unintentional, I couldn't escape the feeling that there's something very Victorian about doing pointless labour when in prison. Like when they used to use the treadmill for punishment – Victorian prisoners were forced to walk on it sometimes for up to ten hours a day for literally no reason other than it would keep them from being 'idle'. Sure, growing vegetables in the fresh air isn't quite as soul-destroying and you land up with a landscaping qualification, but no one wants to feel like their efforts are in vain.

'Growing veg to be composted!' I lamented to my chapel group later that day. 'That is absolutely shocking.'

Three of the ten prison residents who made up our chapel group worked in the gardens. Helen had worked there for over a year and was a little more resigned to this final destination by now. She rolled her eyes at my indignation. 'Compost isn't a complete waste – we're growing veg to make good soil for next year's veg,' she said. I admired her ability to always see the best in a situation that was, anyway, beyond her control – but it wasn't cutting it for me.

'And then what? You can grow excellent compost next year too? We need to write a letter to the governor! This is outrageous.'

Linda sighed. 'Don't get me started. The wing would go mad for it on the canteen but I've been bringing it up at the wing rep meeting and it's a waste of time.' The lack of fresh vegetables was a fairly constant complaint. 'Nothing ever gets changed from the wing rep meetings. They eventually said they couldn't do the veg because there's no one to run it and they thought it would look like favouritism because not every wing has a cooker to cook them.'

'Do you know what, I'm going to go to security,' I said, determined. I didn't want to make extra work for them, but I felt sure I could resolve this. 'Your hard-learnt gardening skills and daily watered leeks cannot go in the bin!'

Linda smiled. She had been there a lot longer than I had and knew that the many cogs of the prison administration were in need of a little oil. Changes plodded through the system as painfully and seemingly never-endingly as the Brexit negotiations.

'Why don't you start collecting it on the sly? They'll assume you're getting gate passes and you can just sneak it out if you can't get one?'

'I don't want to sneak it out!' I responded passionately. The vegetable-based freedom fight was something I actually thought I could win. This was a nice break from the low level but ever-present feelings of inadequacy that had been a feature of my working in the system. Helping to secure proper housing and drugs rehabilitation was often a relentless and losing battle. And our fight against the prison's mental health crisis was, even when armed with the twin ammunitions of glitter and singing, sometimes a fairly fruitless slog. 'I don't want to work around a bad system, I want to change it. Otherwise it'll just be a few of us smuggling out veg, and the rest will still go in the bin. The leeks are the tip of the iceberg (lettuce) – the work of the gardens is under-recognised. Imagine if your vegetables went to a community kitchen and fed people who actually need it! If they're going to get you to work hard and produce amazing vegetables then you deserve them to be seen – to be eaten! It's about empowerment!'

By this point everyone was laughing at me over the top of steaming coffee mugs. 'Go on, girl!' Helen said, punching the air in faux enthusiasm.

I laughed too. 'Well, I'll at least visit security and see what they say.'

In hindsight, my commitment to the leeks was probably a little manic. It was one of a handful of times in my work there that I was losing sight of the point of the whole thing. I'd been told to 'fuck off' one too many times in a day, or made dozens of unanswered phone calls trying to chase the missing results of a resident's cancer scan, or had a week's worth of craft supplies nicked, or watched another person get released without anywhere to go and then come back the next week. I'd come in very hopeful and desperate to challenge the injustices of the prison system, but it hadn't been that simple. Of course it hadn't – otherwise someone would have already done it. They were hardly waiting for an inexperienced graduate writer to come and save the day. The problem was that it was difficult to summarise succinctly on a placard what exactly was wrong. It's difficult to march against a perception or a system, or simply 'the media'. There was no one baddie, no rogue evil officer I could point to as the author of oppression, no uncaring governor; no one we could write to and question why it was that the care system was quite such an effective feeder school for the prison estate, or why so many women in prison were victims of bigger crimes than those they were charged with, and ask if they could please change it.

But leeks! I could certainly rehome leeks and give purpose back to the gardening team. Together we could liberate these magnificent fellows to grace dinner tables throughout the prison and beyond. It was something at least.

Crucially, my leek crusade also received popular support from staff. While they were 70/30 on my side for more non-custodial sentencing for non-violent crimes, the giant leeks were such a splendid sight that everyone felt horrified that they were getting binned.

The following day, I visited Robert's colleague Christoph, who had been harvesting the leeks that morning. He gladly gave me a leek, chopping off the trailing leaves from the top into a neat pale green crop. I promised to use it at the pop-up community café I ran with my friend – and to bring in photos of the meal so the women could see that their leeks were going to good use.

Christoph looked wary. 'You'll have to get a gate pass, mind,' he said.

'Of course! I'm not going to sneak it out,' I explained. 'I'm going to go to security and ask them to sign it off, and while I'm there I'm going to ask about putting together something regular so I can keep using your crops at the community meals.'

Christoph let out an involuntary chuckle. 'Security? They've just had a drugs pass in visits, they've got two people down the seg and they're getting called out over Buscopan twice a day. They're not going to have time to negotiate a veg contract!'

As he spoke, he held open the screen door to a polytunnel so I could pass through. 'But if you're going to spend twenty minutes at security you may as well get some peppers too. The big leeks can be a bit tough anyway; fine for a soup but you need a few extra veg to give it a bit of interest.' He plucked some large red and green peppers from the left-hand side of the aisle and dropped them into the dusty bag-for-life that he'd brought from the office. We emerged from the pepper tunnel and he stopped to peel the muddy outer layers from two huge round Spanish onions which lay on a workbench by the exit. I was ecstatic. I thanked Christoph and proceeded to pack the leek into my rucksack. It was so huge it struggled to fit. Its base left a bulge in the bottom of the bag and the black zips which came either side of the leek's top did not quite meet over the leaves, leaving a small green gap in the middle.

I went to drop my stash of vegetables off at the chapel for safekeeping while I sorted out their release with security. It was, however, too much of a temptation not to pop into some of the neighbouring departments to show friends my oversized haul.

'Bloody hell!' Naomi from the sewing sisters

exclaimed. 'I cannot believe that's a real leek – that is ridiculous.'

Paul, the department's manager, appeared in the doorway to see what the fuss was about. 'That's a good one,' he said. 'Robert's was it? He's known for them.'

'Yep – the residents coached by Robert,' I said. 'I'm taking it to my community café.'

Paul's eyebrows furrowed. 'You need to be careful, Mim – if you get caught going out with that there will be trouble.'

'But it was going in the bin!' I protested. 'And I'm taking it to feed homeless people. Security surely cannot object to that. If it was an official project it would end up as a photo on the boards on the main corridor. Also, I'm going to get a pass, I'm literally on my way there now.'

Paul shook his head warily, but nothing could stop me now. I felt like Sally Hawkins in *Made in Dagenham*. In place of her beehived bob and sewing machine, I was armed with a backpack of soily onions and a can-do attitude.

I had requested a gate pass before to transport pieces of our group's art out to appear in a local exhibition, so technically I knew the process. It had been a bit of a rigmarole. Each art piece had to be checked by the nominee from the Acceptable Activities department, stripped of names and other identifiers, and any offending pieces were removed. Pieces might be deemed offending if they were made by someone too high-profile, or if it had an 'inappropriate theme'. One resident had made a painting where names, statements and lyrics from favourite songs were constructed into the shape of a self-portrait in profile. Children's names swirled together into a ribboned hair bun and place names were written into the neck. Across the bridge of the nose was painted 'I Love Grime' – referring to the east London-based music genre. The tail on the 'G' was not quite distinctive enough, however, and so from some angles it read as 'I Love Crime'. This was deemed inappropriate for obvious reasons, and only allowed out once the resident had given the 'G' an exaggerated tail and an accompanying explanatory note.

After each item had been signed off by Acceptable Activities, it went to be catalogued for a gate pass by security, so that the items could be individually cross-referenced at the gate against this list so as to make sure I was only taking out the allowed items.

It was a process which now conjured up memories of balancing papier-mâché structures, woven rugs and canvases in my arms as I walked along the main corridor, hoping that passing staff would offer to open and lock the gates so I could make my way through the different departments without picking up and setting down the fragile pieces at each one. The whole thing had rather put me off exhibiting anything.

I wondered what the process would be for my vegetables. Would each one be labelled like the artworks? And the inner leaves of the leek checked for scraps of lined paper scribbled with secure data? Or was it a formality?

I unlocked and relocked the gates and then a door into the security department. The department initially looked empty, until I turned the corner and found three people leaning over a desk completing paperwork together.

I said hello and explained, 'I'm here for a gate pass to take out some veg from the gardens.'

All three looked up from what they were doing.

'Sarah, who does gate passes, is out for the day, on training,' one of them responded.

'You'll have to come back.' They all looked back down and carried on filling out the report that was between them on the desk.

'And there's no one else who could sign off a pass?' I asked, interrupting again. 'It's just that I've already picked the veg and I don't want it to go to waste.'

The group looked up again, clearly a little irritated.

'We've got a review coming up so the department is run off its feet. I don't think anyone will be able to help you until later in the week,' the same man responded. Their heads popped down again.

'Right,' I said. 'Do you know who I could speak to about the vegetables from the garden, then? It's just they're all going in the bin because no one wants to trouble you guys with getting gate passes, and it seems a waste of your time that everyone has to come here if they want to take out vegetables.'

Only one of the three looked up this time. 'I know Sarah was trying to sort something else out for gardens but I don't know where it's got to. You'll have to wait until she's back.'

I had already well overstayed my welcome in this reduced, and slightly harassed-looking, department and so I turned, unlocked the door and left, stumped about how to proceed. It was a feature of the prison system that knowing the 'right person' to make things happen was a privilege that you earned, rather than information that was made available to new staff. Officers who had served 20 years acquired extra staff for projects, permission to bring in dogs and security passes for a cafetière, freeing them from the grim realities of instant coffee. No one else ever seemed clear on how they'd done it, however. The first rule of Fight Club, etc. Being a new staff member meant I spent a good deal of time traipsing from department to department, particularly in my first year, trying to find out who could give me permission to put up a new canvas in the hallway or bring in paints, before realising that the wrong person was probably me and my naive enthusiasm, in ignorance of the unofficial codes.

When the new governor arrived, with fresh vision and willing, she invited the bottom-of-the-pile staff to speak directly to her and suddenly progress was a little easier, but that was some time later, and, for now, the vegetables were endangered.

I returned to the chapel to collect the vegetables, resigned to having to smuggle them out instead.

Sian, the pagan chaplain (responsible for the religious input and spiritual wellbeing of the prison's registered pagans), arrived a minute later to find me pushing down the top of the leek with my knee as I struggled to pull the zips on my rucksack shut with both hands. Where the zip had caught the vegetable's flesh it released an oniony smell. Sian was not easily surprised and so glossed over the leek, greeted me warmly and sat down to open her packages from the post pile until I offered the story. Sian was one of my favourite staff in the prison. We bonded over liquorice tea, feminism, a deeply held belief in the sanctity of people and a shared love of Marks and Spencer thermal polo necks. As I described the leek haul and relayed my quest for their freedom, she said, 'I have to tell you, it's not that subtle – I can smell it from here.'

I considered rewrapping the veg in a bin bag to give them a double layer but lunchtime – my window of opportunity – was quickly passing. I had thought it best to take them out while security would be busy checking the staff back in for the afternoon as well as out for their lunch breaks, so I slung my now quite heavy rucksack over my back and headed towards the main gate.

As I scanned my fingerprint to open the cabinet where I had to return my keys, I put the bag down on the floor. Along with the rucksack, I also had the bag-for-life, half-filled with peppers and tomatoes. As I set it down, it slumped over and an onion rolled out. In a panic, I jumped to prop the bag upright as though the escapee heritage onion were a large wrap of heroin. If ever there were evidence that I did not have the skills necessary to smuggle in drugs or phones it was the rate at which my heart beat at the thought of being caught with my prison groceries, and the pace with which I shuffled out of the double gate and towards the car park. Of course, no one batted an eyelid – even at the sharp, stinging smell that filled the reception – and I realised that I was probably being melodramatic and that no one would have cared about my personal rebellion anyway. I deposited the contraband in my car and the rest of the day passed without event.

*

'Can I take a picture of it?' my housemate, Jessie, asked when I arrived back from work.

'With someone holding it for scale?'

'Sure, but don't put it online – it's smuggled goods. I don't want to be Captain Obvious,' I replied, thinking about the guy who'd got arrested after the London riots when he posted a picture of himself surrounded by looted DVDs and Body Shop moisturiser.

'What?' one of my other housemates, Esther, interrupted. 'You never said you weren't allowed it; I thought they gave it to you? I've already uploaded the picture to Instagram from when you came in holding it.'

'Well, yes, they did give it to me, I just wasn't technically supposed to leave the building with it. I thought you said that picture was just for the house WhatsApp,' I responded, a little apprehensive.

She grimaced and said, 'Don't worry, no one knows where it's from. I did think about captioning it, "Courtesy of HMP #HerMassiveProduce" but I thought I probably shouldn't.'

I got my phone out and searched for the post. The caption was harmless ('Massive Leek'), but underneath a friend had commented, 'Wow. Well done, Mim – your gardening has improved since the Uni Allotment Soc days!'

'Oh shit. Everyone's going to think I can actually garden.' I gestured towards my windowsill, where the one remaining plant, after a distinct lack of watering, had started to lie down on its soil bed.

'To be fair, that's *their* assumption; I didn't say you grew it,' Esther responded, liking the friend's comment.

So, as my online reputation as a giant-vegetable gardener gradually and silently grew, we brought the leeks down to the church hall where we ran the community meal, wowing the guests with their size, before chopping them into a stew for the evening meals.

I didn't carry on my short-lived vegetable activism further than another phone call to the security department which yielded no response. But I carried on collecting vegetables that summer, pepper by pepper, onion by onion, giving back a little dignity to the efforts of the gardening team by saving their vegetables from the compost heap. I didn't bring in photos, but I told the gardeners, via the chapel group, about the dishes that we cooked at the café and the hungry mouths that were fed by their daily efforts of planting, weeding, picking and cleaning.

As the crops got depleted much faster than I was taking them, I realised I must have been one of many staff members whose bags were lined with tomatoes, with gate passes and without. It was, again, those unofficial guidelines. Just that no one made quite such a melodrama about it as I did.

*

(It's worth noting that this is a thing of the past! The prison has a new governor now, and last week at my now full-time community café we received a large box of onions grown in the prison, dropped off by one of the through-the-gate staff. We chopped and cooked them with one of the women, now released, who volunteers with us. It felt like fucking progress.)

THREE USES FOR PRISON COFFEE WHITENER

1. **CHEESECAKE**

   I'm told when mixed with the cream cheese from the canteen it's almost like the real thing.

2. **BREAD TOPPER**

   Much like sprinkle-topped bread, or a poor man's doughnut, a sprinkling of sweetened whitener over your bread will turn it into a pudding.

3. **GLUE**

   If you've run out of Blu Tack for your notice board, dab a little whitener in some water and it will do the job.

   NB: It is not an equivalent for dry shampoo.

DORA THE EXPLORER

The traffic of the prison is much more varied than you might imagine. Alongside the officers you might find suited Jehovah's Witness chaplains completing daily checks of the segregation unit, a pink-haired writer running the reading group, shiny-bobbed librarians ordering in legal information, the wiry yoga teacher laying out her mats in the chapel, white-haired volunteer visitors coming to see lifers whose other visits have petered out, suited examiners to assess the hairdressing class, and retired ladies serving teas and chocolate bars to the residents' friends and families in the visiting hall. But never was there such contrast to the grey gates as when Dora visited.

Dora was on first glance a rather unlikely pick for a prison volunteer. She was five foot tall, in her sixties, spoke with a singsong Scottish accent and helped to run the chapel groups. Like a doting grandma she always brought biscuits and little trinkety gifts for me and my colleagues that she'd picked up in the charity shop on her way. She wore those scarves that look like hairy rainbows – multi-coloured and knitted from fibrous wool – and practical purple jersey trousers with white trainers. On hearing one of the women confess to a romantic liaison with someone on their wing, she'd trill in her lilting Glaswegian tones, 'Oh deear me! I hoope yurr not getting invoolved in any nortiness? Any hanky-panky? That wouldnae do at all!'

And yet Dora, so at odds with the prison's regulated clothing and boundaried interactions, was one of the most beloved volunteers you could imagine. In fact, it was probably because she was so unfazed by the formalities and frameworks we all operated under that Dora was such a hit. The postcards she brought in showing puppies poking out from flowerpots were so popular that they even survived pad moves; being taken down from notice boards, transported and then re-pinned on the new board. Her motherly advice, which from anyone else would elicit eye-rolling, was taken with good grace. After listening to the group indulge in one of its regular moaning sessions, for example, she was the kind of person to suggest that we all name three things we were thankful for instead, and obediently we all did. There were many things that made Dora hard not to love. My favourite was that she once told me, giggling, that she always adds three kisses to the bottom of all her texts, 'one for the Father, one for the Son, and one for the Holy Spirit'!

There are, however, both perks and challenges to having a volunteer who did not fit cleanly into the prison's ways of existing. One Thursday she arrived later than usual for our afternoon group – she tended to arrive 45 minutes before the start to set up the teas and arrange biscuits on the few flowered plates that could be found among the plastic ones in the chapel's kitchen. I was called to go and meet her by the gate: volunteers can't carry keys and so have to be collected by staff members who can lead them through the gates and doors and stay with them in case they need to be let into a loo or out of an emergency exit.

As soon as I arrived I knew she was in a fluster; her fringe was sticking to her forehead and her face was a light pink.

'They asked me why I was in the loo!' she warbled, looking a little panicked and not making much sense. 'I had tae put my bag in the locker – I came oan the bus. And the chestnuts werrr for you!'

Wanting to avoid a scene in the prison's entrance hall, I ushered her out into the deliveries courtyard and started heading towards the chapel.

'What do you mean they asked you why you were in the loo?' I asked. 'Who's "they"?'

Dora linked my arm with hers: a cosy gesture which made me feel conspicuous next to the black-clothed officers who always kept an appropriate distance from each other.

'I was just collecting chestnuts from the tree by the bus stop,' she enthused. 'You gurrls are so busy I thought you wouldnae manage to stop for them before they're goone.'

She was right. Chestnut foraging was rarely on my mind after a long morning in the classroom.

I let us both into the chapel, still unsure as to what had caused the upset, and locked the door behind us.

'A lady officer was knocking on the loo door,' she continued, 'quite irate she was! Saying, "What are you doing in there? You cannae be in this block," but I had an upset tum so couldnae come oot right away. I told her so but she kept banging.'

The wall of lockers where staff and volunteers can put their possessions before coming into the prison shares a building with the staff gym, where officers train over their lunch break. A woolly-scarved lady pottering around with chestnuts, it seemed, had aroused suspicion. Dora's brow furrowed, and she handed me and my colleague a Tesco carrier bag half-full of chestnuts. 'When I came out she asked me what I was doing there and why I had chestnuts. I told her they were for my gurrls and she looked quite alarmed. Quite rrrude she was!' Dora exclaimed, the 'r's in rude rolling as she did. 'Treating me leeke an intruder!'

Dora was, of course, harmless, and someone getting their knickers in a twist over chestnuts would ordinarily not worry me, but Dora had previous. She'd been seen initiating a hug with one of the residents on the landing which, for good reason, was not allowed. But she was bidding farewell to someone who was about to be released. Unfortunately, they'd embraced in full sight of the officer who was coordinating the evening movement. Thankfully, the officer had chosen not to make anything of it, but for the week after I had the niggling worry that it would come back to haunt her and I'd made it clear to her that if she didn't toe the line, we might not be allowed to have her back in.

There was also the time before that when she'd been found with a glass bottle during a bag search and responded, 'Whoopsee, silly Dora!' to the unimpressed officer who was trying to impress on her the severity of such a slip.

'I hope I havenae caused you bother again!' Dora said, sighing.

'Not to worry, Dora,' I replied, trying to reassure her. 'We'll just make sure they know the chestnuts were for us. Let's forget about it and get on with filling the

Thermos flasks.' Dora became immediately cheerful. 'I've bought some wee choccy wafers in from B&M.' She opened the packet and began pouring them onto the plate to join the Bourbons from our group supply.

I unlocked the supplies cupboard so that Dora could refill the sugar bowl for the table, as was routine.

'I won't put too much in!' she said, counting out teaspoons into the bowl. Like all good grandmas, Dora was a feeder and liked to fill up the bowls to their brim. We had to crack down, though, after someone was caught filling their bra with it. (Quite cleverly, they'd done it during prayer time, using the opportunity of our closed eyes to both package up and stow away their loot.)

Dora had by this time calmed down enough to have me in stitches over her review of *Naked Attraction*, the dating game show on Channel 4 involving nude contestants. 'Thiy reveal their private parts! A geentleman yisterday evun suggested he preferred a leedy with less hair!' she gestured downwards. 'What a wuurld we live in!' she finished, shaking her head. Our conversation was interrupted by a flow of people walking past the chapel window, which signalled the first throes of afternoon movement. Thursdays, when the chapel group took place, was a visits day, so the first lot of walkers were always heading towards the visiting hall. You can tell because they are each wearing their own version of Sunday best. Prison greys – the grey tracksuits available to every resident – are conspicuously absent, replaced by pristine borrowed branded tracksuits, jeans, dresses or even a special 'visits outfit' which is kept packed away, only to be brought out for those occasions. Hair is straightened with the wing's straighteners (borrowed by handing in your key fob to the office) and Avon makeup is worn (if you have private cash and the right privileges; otherwise it is borrowed from friends or improvised with cigarette ash – back before cigarettes were banned – or red and black pencils smuggled back from the education department). I always liked to watch this group walk past the window, dressed for the occasion, absenting themselves from life inside for an afternoon of snacks from the visitors' kiosk, wearing borrowed tops and tights. For us, though, the visits parade was mostly observed as a time marker; principal movement happened after visits, so it meant that it was almost time to collect our cohort from the main corridor to escort them to the chapel.

It was not long into the group's session when a call came through from security. The managing chaplain waved me back into the office through the metal-reinforced glass window in the door while we were still on biscuits and an introductory round.

'It's security on the phone,' he said, looking at me curiously. 'Someone's reported Dora for bringing in gifts for the residents.' I must have looked worried because he added, 'It'll be fine, just explain.'

I picked up the phone gingerly.

'It's Callum calling from the security department,' the man on the other end of the phone said. 'I'm just following up a query to do with an incident in the officers' gym earlier today. Is it something you're already aware of?'

I told him it was. 'It's not a disciplinary action,' he continued, 'we just need to keep an eye on these things, investigate them thoroughly. If you could tell me what the chapel volunteer was doing in the gym that would help clear things up.'

'She comes on the bus,' I replied, 'so she needs to use the lockers for her phone and things.' Dora actually came on three buses. She lived in a small town and made a two-hour journey on public transport both ways to get to us each week.

'And why was she upstairs?'

'She needed the loo,' I explained.

It was, I thought, quite an indignity that whatever overzealous officer had reported her had felt the need to chase her out of the loo anyway, so I was pleased when the security officer replied, 'Oh right, of course, no problem. It's really just these chestnuts, then, that's an issue. The woman herself – Dora, did you say her name was? – when questioned by the officer said she was bringing them in to give to the girls.'

I rather liked the idea that they thought Dora was

smuggling contraband chestnuts into the wings to be roasted on contraband lighters.

'The girls is us: me and my colleague. She's already given them to us to take home.'

'Ah, right, okay,' he replied, satisfied. 'Well, like I said, just part of the job to check these things out.'

'Of course, no problem,' I replied, putting down the phone and returning to the group.

The prison, as ever, was more human, more flexible and understanding than I would have given it credit for. I made the mistake, when I arrived, of thinking of it as an unwieldy institution, a machine that processed those who had broken the law. But, like any other institution, it is just a collection of people. Empathetic, flawed, kind, frustrated people working within an ever-adapting framework of law and policy. A framework which held incongruously between its struts: Dora and her biscuits and scarves, SO Callum following up on staff concerns, HR administrators with six grandchildren and young Lycra-ed yoga teachers, visiting examiners and dedicated volunteers. It held families waiting in the visitors' centre, young officers learning the ropes, and older ones who'd paced the corridors for 20 years; the naive and the wise and well worn.

I returned to the group and Dora greeted me with a smile, a box of white chocolate fingers and a stack of her encouraging Bible bookmarks. 'I hope you don't mind,' she said. 'We ran out of the wafers and I thought they'd like to try these – white chocolate, they are! Christmas special.'

She opened the packet and passed them around the group, then exclaimed, as she always did, 'I cannae tell ye what a pleasure it is to be here with you all. I believe we're going to have a blessed afternoon!'

CONVERSATIONS FROM CUSTODY

IN THE CLASSROOM:

Me: So quilling just involves coiling these strips of paper into different pictures. You can use the templates on the table or make up your own design – be creative!

[30 minutes later, Kim shows me an intricately quilled design of an erect penis]

Kim: I thought I'd do my own design rather than the template. Underneath I'm going to write, 'Love you, you big wanker' and send it to my best friend.

AT A POETRY-SHARING SESSION:

Resident 1: My arms were heavy, my feet were numb I'm sorry that I stabbed you, Mum

[Silence]

Resident 2: You stabbed your mum?

Resident 3: [Shrugs and says to Resident 1 sympathetically] I stabbed my boyfriend.

SHOUTED OUT OF THE WINDOW OF THE HEALTHCARE BLOCK TO OUR TEAM:

Resident: YOU'VE ALL GOT SATAN IN YOU!

Alice: [Shrugs] She says that to everyone. Don't take it personally.

IN THE CLASSROOM:

Resident 1: I could hear the two in the pad above me shagging all night. Really loud.

[**Me:** subtly writes down the names to report it later]

Resident 2: Miss, have you just wrote down the names so you can dob them in?

Me: Er. Yes. I have actually.

TALES FROM THE GAME:

Tale 1: Fucking perverts, some of those judges. One had me tying him up and sucking his toes and then slammed me in court a couple of months later. Eighteen months for shoplifting.

Tale 2: I had one who used to pump up my arse with a balloon pump and then get me to fart in his face – £400 an hour.

Tale 3: It's not any different in the dance clubs. You still get scruffy men coming over you when you're halfway through a lap dance. That's why we've got the PVC shorts. They're wipe clean.

GLOSSARY 3

ADJUDICATION An in-prison court process. More commonly called a 'nicking' – for example, 'I got nicked for swearing at an officer.' When a resident has been caught doing something they shouldn't, different parties give evidence and they're brought before the governor to explain themselves. Punishments are 'loss of' something, such as having your TV and association time taken away or being downgraded to 'basic'. In more serious cases, extra days may be added to your sentence. Sometimes you might get all three.

BULLY BOOK Officially called a 'Challenging Behaviour Document', a bully book is where staff write down comments about a resident's behaviour. It's not unlike being put on behaviour report at school – if you've been rude or you're caught picking on someone, for example, then you get put on report. If you're on a bully book you also have to go without privileges, like having a TV, so it's in your interest to collect good comments in the book to be presented as evidence when your file is reviewed, then, hopefully, you get taken off it.

CO-ACCUSED/CO-DEFENDANT This is the person you were accused of doing your crime with. If you and a friend got caught carrying out a robbery together, they'd be your co-accused. If you're on remand and haven't had your trial yet, then ideally (for the prosecution, at least) you'd not be on the same wing as your 'co', so that you don't have time to confer before the trial date. The ugly sister of 'co-accused' is the dreaded 'joint enterprise'. This is when, for example, you might have been on the scene when someone was murdered, and because you were part of the general goings-on of the evening you get convicted of murder too under 'joint enterprise', even if you never touched or spoke to the victim. Joint enterprise is particularly used in gang convictions where seven people might be found guilty of one murder.

LISTENERS A resident who is trained in professional listening. This is a privileged position – a bit like an in-house Samaritans service. Listeners are residents who are trained up to hear people's concerns and problems and signpost/advocate. Residents can call a listener at any point, whether they're on bang-up (when you're locked in your pad), or at 3am, and they'll come and visit you. They are like the guardian angels/big sisters of the prison population.

MDT (MANDATORY DRUGS TEST) These happen sporadically and without prior warning. If a resident fails one of these it could mean losing privileges. Not all drug use shows up on these, though, particularly new innovations.

ON REMAND When the resident has been charged but they're still awaiting trial. They can be 'remanded on bail' or 'bailed', where they spend their remand time living at home, or 'remanded in custody', where they spend it in jail. If they're then found guilty and they've already been in prison on remand, they get their remand time taken off their sentence. If their remand time has already been longer than their sentence then they get awarded 'time served' and can leave straight from court. If they're remanded in custody but are then found not guilty, they got a very raw deal.

Unlike other prisoners, remand prisoners can still vote; they also get more visits and more private cash.

PALS LINE The number residents call if they're ill and need to book an appointment or be allowed the day off work. There is a phone or two on each wing.

RELEASE ON TEMPORARY LICENCE (ROTL – PRONOUNCED 'ROTTLE') If your main source of prison information is American TV dramas, then ROTL is similar to 'furlough'. If you're granted ROTL then it means you can leave temporarily. Some people get it one-off for 'special purposes' like a funeral or a marriage, but going out for the day can also be part of your resettlement plan. People can have ROTL a few times a week to enable them to sort out housing or start a volunteering placement or get some training so they're more ready for release.

They're a pretty great idea, because it means that people are more prepared for life outside once they get there, particularly if they've served a long time. I know one guy in his twenties who went inside prison in the mid-noughties and got out in 2015. Because he'd almost completely missed the growth of the internet and the rise of the smart phone, he struggled to get his head around it all when he emerged out the other side of the system – where he promptly freaked out over a satnav. ROTL gets people back into normal life a little more gradually. There is though, quite predictably, a lot of boxes you have to tick to be ROTL eligible, and then a lot more paperwork before it actually happens.

TREATMENTS This gets called about three times per day to send residents to collect their medication. Some people are allowed medication 'in possession', which means that they get a week's prescription and can keep it in their cell. To reduce the risk of overdose, misuse (i.e. smoking instead of swallowing) and pills being traded, most tablets are given out daily by a nurse who will check the resident in question has swallowed them.

Methadone is dispensed to recovering heroin addicts separately at lunchtime. When methadone is called, a long line forms in the corridor to collect small plastic shot glasses with varying amounts of the bright green viscous liquid from a hatch next to the seg. Everyone is encouraged to reduce their prescription while they're in, so as to gradually withdraw from the opiates. You'd often see someone looking a bit rough because they'd 'come down 5ml'.

VIVIAN: A GUEST CHAPTER

[Transcribed from an interview with Vivian Carr, ex prison resident]

It's terrifying when you first get in there. I remember walking up the corridor with my two bin bags they gave me. One has your diary in, your papers in. The other has a quilt in and two pillows. And you get your greys – that's your grey tracksuit bottoms. They gave me a pair of Kappa trainers back then, brand new. I thought, *Bloody hell, I love it, where am I at?*

Then I started to see the girls come out. You know the girls who have been in for a lot longer. They've overcome their drug habits, they're putting the weight on, they've learnt the jail talk; the lingo. You get told on the way in, 'Don't give anything away and don't borrow anything', but you don't get nothing for the first two weeks you're in there. You used to get a special pack. It was a half ounce of baccy, a ten-pence chew bar, and, I dunno, some Rizlas and matches. It takes two weeks to get your canteen sorted. Any money you get sent in.

Anyway, so you carry your bags up the corridor and then the minute you open those double doors to go into the main jail you hear the intense volume of everything. It's the noise of it, the speed of it, the smell – like a hospital. There can be a bell going off and you're seeing five screws running that way, two coming from A wing, and two coming the other way from H wing towards two lasses pulling hair and fucking punching each other, do you know what I mean? Shouting up the landing, gates banging. From there, you get took onto the wings and get told which wing you're going on. I looked down one wing and a girl was standing there, pulled her pants down. They were doing the floors, scrubbing, and she just pulled them down. Her mates burst out laughing. I went that red! I thought, *Fuck me, where am I?* It's full of problems with mental health. To see all that – it's very intimidating. I'm not a fighter, I never have been. I couldn't fight my way out of a paper bag. I'm a very soft-natured person. Soft-natured but I'm also physically weak . . . the minute I saw blood I would be stopping, you know?

Oh, I forgot this bit. When you get in, if you want to still get your medications you got prescribed outside then you had to pee in a bottle. They'd tell you to hold your hands in the air so they know you're not messing about with a spare bottle. Well, one hand in the air – you needed the other for holding the bottle. But they're at the door literally saying, 'Have you been yet? Have you been yet?' And you can't pee because they're there and you've still got one hand sticking up! But they'll also warn you: 'If you don't pee in that bottle you won't get no meds' – so you have to stand there for ten or 15 minutes, them talking all the time, until you can finally get a little bit of pee out and hand that over.

I got put on B wing, which was the YO [young offenders] wing back then, 'cause I was 17. I'm thinking, *I'm going to be okay here.* At least I don't have to mix with anyone older. I'm 34 now. It's not like the first time anymore but it's still terrifying. For me it is. I'm a social person but you're surrounded by people you wouldn't mix with. That you wouldn't go out of your way to see. You do your best.

The thing was, you were supposed to fight back. They used to say to me, 'You make yourself a victim because you don't stand up for yourself. You've got to learn to be like, "Fuck off, I'm not giving you nowt."' Instead I'd say, 'Oh yeah, you can have a rollie', pass them the baccy pouch and get it handed back with half the baccy gone. They'd take a clump out and hide it, you know?

I guess in their minds they thought, *If she's dumb enough to pass it . . .*

On B wing, we'd go out on movement before the other wings. It was more so we didn't mix with older prisoners and stuff. There was one girl. She thought she ruled the wing. Everyone would run about to appease her, fill her fucking flask up. Last time I was in, a couple of days before I got out, one of my tops got ripped up. It was this lass. I was supposed to be saving my medication for her but because I never gave her anything and she was a washer lady my top was ripped to fuck. I said to the screw, 'Can I get some washing-up tablets because if my washing's going down there it's not coming back properly?' I got this new Karrimor fleece off my dad. I didn't dare put it in the wash so I never washed it the whole time I was in. I thought, *Nah. That's going to go.* My Nike tracksuit was the same.

Oh God, I remember there was a woman on the first sentence who came in who was absolutely done in when she arrived, must have been sold, you know, passed about. You knew it was something awful like that but she couldn't talk much about it. She used to just lie in her bed and wet herself. The screws would humiliate her, pull her mattress out – 'Get that fucking scruff out of here, she's pissed the bed.' It frightened me the way they talked.

And that song came out that goes, 'It's getting hot in here, so take off all your clothes.' And when I've walked on the landing and there's male screws all together singing that song – I thought, *Fucking hell, it's going to be bent.* They weren't actually going to touch you in that way but it's what you're used to, you know?

There was a few who were like that, though. The day I got out of prison an officer met me on the bus. Said, 'You're one of our girls, aren't you? Fancy a pint?' Very dirty man. Now, he went with a lot of prisoners. Told me he resigned as soon as they put the cameras in.

He was one of those where people would slash up and sit in the door with blood all over themselves and he'd say, 'You're all right now, aren't you? Go to bed.' He'd say, 'There's that much paperwork we won't bother reporting it.' You block a toilet now and they have to fill paperwork in. But the screws are just normal people, you know?

I remember two lads working there – broad, aggressive lads, my boyfriend knows them. I remember they broke up a fight once and, because the lass wouldn't stop doing what she was doing, one of them whacked her head off the pipes, you know, the ones along the pads? I thought, *Bloody hell, that's a bit much.*

There's a lot of favouritism. The loudest ones are better known. I think they get more attention – they get the mental health officers out, they get the treatment. If you're quiet you disappear into the background. Which is what I wanted to do, really.

There are some brilliant officers too. I remember once I was getting bullied by two lasses who slapped me straight on the landing. They were from London so I didn't always understand what they were saying. What it was, they fancied the pad-mate I was with. She would openly admit, 'I'm petrified, I'm not even gay. I'm doing what I'm doing just to get along.'

She kissed both of them but that's as far as it went. But the abuse they would shout out the window at me because of it! 'Vivian, you best not be touching my lass!' It was funny because *they* were both sharing her, and I wasn't gay either. It wasn't nice. I felt sorry for her, but the minute she got in front of them she'd change as well. She only done that for her own survival, I understand that now.

Anyway, I can remember borrowing a tape off one of those girls who was bullying me and then I got moved out of that pad because of the abuse that was getting shouted in. I couldn't say anything to them because I was scared, so in a weird personal way of standing up to them I thought, *Fuck this, I'm taping over it*, and I did. But I would still see her in the dining hall, so when she came and said, 'If you don't find my tape, I'm going to knock the fuck out of you,' I realised I shouldn't have done it.

I was fucking terrified. So one of the screws on the wing knew about it and brought a tape in, his own tape. He knew that I couldn't report it properly because I'd get it even worse, so he just brought a tape in for me to give to her. That's what I mean, you get officers who can see that's not your nature, that you're not a fighter, and they'll help you. There's a lot of women and men who will sit down and talk to you.

That was the first time I went in, though; it's better now. It's changed. Same people, though. The last time I was in, I bumped into this girl from Glasgow. I hadn't seen her since my last sentence. She said, 'Fucking hell. Are you still in?' And I was like, 'I haven't been for years. I'm only here for shoplifting.' Always the same faces. I got six weeks on my last sentence. Or really I got three months and then served six weeks.

I feel so sorry for the shy girls. On that sentence there was one girl in who looked ill. I approached the screws and I said, 'That girl hasn't seen a meal for months.' She was stick thin. Suffered mental health. The reason was, she got picked on in dining hall. I seen her get punched, the screw seen her get punched, and nobody done nowt about it. They liked the lass that punched her. It's a bit bent like that. I know you do more for people you like, I get that, but not in that role. You're meant to be . . . you know. There's a lot of good officers there that have left because of rule changes, different governors, and the cuts.

*

I've read about a boy who was buying MDMA, a posh boy from a private school, and what he got off on – and this wouldn't ever work for me in court – was this. He said, 'Listen, we all sort of chipped in and I was just holding them for everyone.' It worked! He walked straight out of court because he could afford a good lawyer and was from a good family. Having said that, when I had a solicitor, I was absolutely blown away that someone would get up and argue for me. He said, 'I know you've got issues with your drugs and mental health but I'm on your side.'

People definitely come out worse than they went in. You learn more about how to conceal drugs; people tell you stories about what they've done, how they've got away with it, what to say when you get locked up. So it's an education. Especially if you've got that personality where you'll go out of your way to please people. I'm a people-pleaser. I know for a fact I am. I'm also a bit of a chameleon. I can change who I am to fit in with people, but I don't fit in with the loud, violent, aggressive. I'm not into bullying, can't stand it. There are nice lasses but it's just the people that are there – you can't help learning more about breaking the law because that's all they talk about.

I think there should be more support surrounding

mental health – Mind, Samaritans, you lot, all these other ones that give support, counselling. Proper refuges so you can get away from partners who batter you and have you on the game, and don't have to go miles away to a place full of drink with no carpets.

You know, I've been on medication for my mental health that many years that last time I went to the doctor he said, 'What do you think you should be on?' Not like it normally is when you say how you're feeling and they tell you what you need – he was asking me! Ha!

He didn't give it me all, though; he said I was pushing my luck a bit at the end. He said, 'It's not happening – I'll give you one out of two. You'll have to be happy with that.'

You know, even without drugs I've got these voices in my head telling me I'm worthless, that I'm nothing. My dad was violent and we grew up in and out of refuges – and now my partner's violent. He calls me a fat slag every day. After a while you believe it, don't you? I want it all to change, but I don't feel good enough to be around decent people sometimes . . .. well, all the time really.

I couldn't tell you what would solve it but good accommodation is a start. Having a door you can lock and be safe. And more people like yous lot. I can't thank you enough. What you lot have done for my mental health. My dad's been over the moon with it, saying, 'You look good now – you can tell you've not been abusing drugs daily.'

I came out with a house because of my boyfriend. That's one of the reasons I've stayed with him because he's someone to get out to. Otherwise you get a letter saying you've got 18 days to go to the council, and if you get somewhere it's never near anywhere you know; it's a town where rent's cheap and it's full of prostitutes and crackheads. I can't be around that, me. Otherwise – I admit it – it starts seeming like that's normal and I get into it and then realise how far I've slipped down.

For me, accommodation is a big thing. Our landlord has left sewage coming through the ceiling, most of the rooms are locked off 'cause they're too damp and the door gets kicked in every week by people robbing us or wanting drugs. I couldn't keep it clean if I wanted to. I'm massively depressed in the house I'm in. But now I'm in a lot of debt. If I can't find another place it's going to be hard to walk away from this life and, my partner – he's broke my jaw, you know? The house is a nightmare. It sounds stupid but it makes me miss being inside.

I had this friend in there, Lindsey. People thought we were related we were that close, and I'd never had a friendship like that. It wasn't like with lads who want to use you and come round with six cans and run off with your Giro. She was mint . . . It was lovely. I miss the friendships. I wasn't allowed to meet back up with her after we got out. I found her on Facebook but my boyfriend wouldn't let me. It's harder out here to meet people. She was going through the same things as me. She was keeping a low profile, hiding in her room. She used to say to me, 'You've got a contagious laugh.' I'd burst out laughing, then she'd burst out laughing and the electric would end up getting turned off because we were laughing that hard that the full wing could hear. Some of my best times were in there. Her mum was even sending me cards saying, 'Thanks for helping her.'

In some ways you're safer in there than out here. Once you're locked behind your door. But once your door opens you're surrounded by lots of people's problems.

I did art when I was in; they set me up a college course for when I got out. But I messed up that one. I won't lie, I'm trying my best but I've had a slip-up here and there.

I'll always be an addict. Doesn't matter how long I'm clean, I'm always going to be an addict, aren't I? I think it'll get easier over time, not harder. It sounds full of myself but you know what I'm really looking forward to? I want to help people. I admit it. I want to be a part of society.

I'll tell you what it is. Last year everybody thought a bomb had been left in a carrier bag outside the second-hand shop and the police evacuated the whole street except for our house because they knew the kind of people who lived there. They didn't even knock on our door. And I thought, *Fucking hell, that's what people think of us?* You know what I mean? Worthless. Not even worth a knock. That was an eye-opener. I don't want to have that relationship with the police. They might have had to go to a house that morning after attending a crash and tell someone their son's not coming back. You don't know what they've dealt with before seeing you. But they keep going. We'd be lost without them.

WHO GOVERNS THE GOVERNOR: A SHORT RANT

In 2008, a photo was published in the *Sun* of some Holloway prison residents dressed up and slathered in fake blood for a Halloween party. It was a long-termer wing and included, among others, a handful of people who were in for murder. It was, it has to be said, a giant cock-up and in subsequent years has become an oft-cited case study in bad PR, still striking fear into the heart of anyone authorising a prison event. Lest we forget the public bollocking the Holloway staff received and the prison party ban imposed afterwards by Justice Secretary, Jack Straw. The watchful eye of the press, though, goes far beyond the obvious culprit of prison parties.

Whether it's an art exhibition, a drug recovery celebration or a visiting educational theatre group – 'You've got to ask yourself,' one member of the Acceptable

Activities Committee explained to me, 'what your event would look like if it was a headline in the *Daily Mail*.' Given that the *Daily Mail* is able to spin off critical headlines merely for the crime of being a politician in a skirt or a child fleeing war, it does rather put a dampener on innovative rehabilitation projects, particularly if you were hoping they'd be funded by the public purse rather than by my constant cap-in-hand charity fundraising.

Even the prison's lunch menu is subject to 'freedom of information' requests. As such, the Christmas lunch is 'turkey and accompaniments' – so the *Sun* doesn't find out that the prison has stretched to pigs in blankets and run the headline: 'Convicts treated to Christmas banquet while hardworking Brits face budget Christmas', or similar. As though knowing that people in prison are having a shit Christmas lunch provides more comfort for the factory workers in Sheffield rather than, I don't know, being paid a living wage.

If you're a member of the press, rest assured – being in prison isn't nice. It also isn't that good at rehabilitating people, because politicians don't want to look like they're putting money into the prison system rather than the NHS. At the risk of ranting, it's about time we acknowledge that both of these institutions deal with our national health.

LET'S TALK ABOUT SEX, BABY

We talked about sex a lot in the prison. It's the not-having-it that made it such a hot topic, I guess.

Of course, it wasn't everyone not having it: we had plenty of lesbians who had secret relationships, and plenty of others who referred to themselves as 'jail-bent' or 'gay for the stay'. But there were many others for whom prison was a frustrating opportunity to practise some involuntary celibacy.

In the classroom there was gossip about who was shagging their pad-mate: the tell-tale sounds carried to the other cells through the heating pipes which connected the network of rooms like a string-and-tin-can telephone. Or there were detailed explanations of what someone was planning when they were reunited with a partner after their release.

There was a darker side, too. Stories of sex shared in

quieter moments over mugs of instant coffee. Stories that told less of choice and more of the touches of adult hands before it was understood what they meant. Accounts where the idea of withholding your body from someone who wanted it was seen as equally impossible in adult life as it had been for the bruised little girls who'd first learnt that other people felt entitled to their bodies. Uncles, siblings, foster carers, parents, family friends and strangers – strangers who'd selected them from children's homes and who, in the absence of the watchful eye of a caring parent or guardian nearby, had groomed them fast and young. And now it was drug dealers and partners who used their bodies – not only for themselves but given out to others, earning enough to support two habits.

There was one chapel group where, because of various appointments and visits, the group – usually five – was that day just me, Ellie and Hannah. They'd both been in the chapel group for some time so we knew each other well. I'd had Ellie in the classroom and chapel through two sentences. She was, in a busy chapel group, often the one who drove me up the wall: wandering about the chapel pinching biros and talking over other, shyer members of the group, but that day, she sat quietly listening to Hannah ask me questions about my experience of sex – namely, that I hadn't had any. My boyfriend and I had decided to wait until we were engaged to sleep together.

'You're not missing much,' Hannah said, taking a handful of Bourbons from the plate I'd just topped up. 'I mean, it's not really for us anyway, is it? Have we not got any chocolate digestives?!' The two questions flowed into one, as though the lack of digestives and the lack of sexual satisfaction were both fairly unremarkable facts of life. 'I had one partner I did enjoy it with – the kids' dad,' she continued. 'But I mostly just liked that it made him happy.'

'What they show in the films is bollocks,' Ellie added, spooning coffee granules into her mug and then adding water from the Thermos. 'They want it all the time, no matter if you're up for it. A couple of times I've woken up at a party and I've known that someone has had sex with me but didn't know who. Dirty buggers. There's none of that in *The Notebook*.'

'Ellie,' I replied, shocked, 'if someone has sex with you without your permission, that's rape.'

She paused for a moment as if to process the suggestion, and then shook her head. 'Oh no, it wasn't rape. I was out of it from the drugs. It's like my foster carer used to say' – she put on a Hyacinth Bucket trill – '"If you keep putting yourself in these situations then you've only got yourself to blame." I was lucky really – I used to pass out at parties all the time; something really bad could have happened to me.'

I wondered whether to insist that something really

bad *had* happened, that it *was* rape. To tell her that she should be outraged, that we should investigate further, but the words stuck in my throat. I wrestled with the thought that this new realisation might only add to the trauma.

Hannah broke the silence. 'You'll enjoy it, though, Mim, 'cause it'll be with someone you love.' She paused a long moment and then continued with a dampened voice, 'I'm not sure I could enjoy it now, even like that.' Her now-quiet voice crumbled and was suddenly interrupted with a sharp intake of breath. 'What happened when I was a kid,' she explained, 'I think it fucked it up for me. I don't even care who I have sex with now.'

Later, I could not dislodge the story from my head. Hannah's story paired itself in my thoughts with Maya Angelou's description of abuse in *I Know Why the Caged Bird Sings*. 'Then there was the pain,' Maya writes, 'a breaking and entering when even the senses are torn apart. The act of rape on an eight-year-old body is a matter of the needle giving because the camel can't. The child gives, because the body can, and the mind of the violator cannot.'[11]

Brain pathways – you learn in the prison's training on trauma awareness – are formed hard and young. Our

---

[11] Maya Angelou, *I Know Why the Caged Bird Sings*, Virago: 1984, p.78.

survival instinct tells us that the surest path to safety is not to resist someone stronger, more powerful or more aggressive. So, when attacked, our innate desire to stay alive takes the strength out of struggling arms and kicking legs. It saps our muscles of their power to fight back and stops our mouths from screaming so that we make it through with minimal physical harm. Our brain learns that if we fight back, we'll get hurt even more. And, each time you make it through an attack alive, this non-resistance is further embedded into your survival instincts. And so, as the stories have always gone, abuse begets abuse.

'You can't hold onto it, though,' Hannah said. She had tears in her eyes by this point but they were joined by a determined look, and her voice reassembled itself into a continuous thread, thickening as she spoke. 'I thought I could never forgive him. Being in here, you realise it: we're all so fucking full of bitterness. But holding onto the anger makes you the victim. It eats you away. I'm not his victim anymore. He got to choose what happened back there, but it was me that chose to forgive him. I got to make the decision. I did.'

That was one of those days when, after the patrol officer had led them away, I cried hard, crouched on the chapel office's carpet-tiled floor so that I could not be seen from the large windows: tears which felt inappropriate, that I knew were not mine to cry. But I cried at

Hannah's resilience, and because I didn't know how else to respond to such a depth of pain. And I cried in awe of her forgiveness because it was the closest thing to courage I'd ever seen. It was a courage that was the opposite of submission. It felt more powerful than the brute force which had demanded it. I wished I could collect it and distil it down in a shot. It would be like those thick green millilitres of methadone in plastic cups which settled itching hands and frustrated bones. Her forgiveness was one which settled swirling thoughts and shaking limbs into a calm, focused clarity.

Of course, it could not be distilled, even less taught: it was a thing hard-earned.

SIX USES FOR SANITARY PRODUCTS[12]

1. Tampons can be shredded up and stuffed into a lighter which has run out of gas, where it will ignite and produce a flame.
2. Sanitary towels can be stuck along window openings to be used as draught excluders.
3. Tampons can be crushed at the end and used as makeup brushes. The shape is particularly effective for blusher or bronzer.
4. Sanitary towels can be stuck to the soles of shoes and to hands and shuffled around on as a very effective way to clean floors and windows.

---

[12] Sanitary products being unlimited in prison.

5. Sanitary towels can be used as insoles in no-longer-comfortable shoes.

6. Both sanitary towels and tampons can be torn apart and the cotton wool inside used as either earplugs, fake snow or makeup remover pads.

THE INTERNATIONAL
WOMEN'S DAY FIGHT

We were told about the arrival of the new governor some months before the incumbent was due to retire. A change of number one governor can bring about a big shift for a prison. It's almost like a change in prime minister, in that they bring not only a new flavour, new focus and priorities but also a rejig of the other governors, and a new deputy. Apart from knowing that we were about to – hurrah – have a woman running our women's prison (and a female deputy too), I knew very little about her.

There were, of course, rumours. Chief among them: that she was 'for the prisoners'.

This statement held a completely different meaning depending on who was saying it and what tone they used. The implication of the second half of the sentence could either be 'as opposed to the officers' (a criticism) or 'rather than against them' (a compliment).

In the end she was a pleasant surprise. She started by visiting every department to see what was going on and where we were falling down. It was, after a year working in the prison, the first conversation I'd had with a number one.

Our previous number one, and I assume most others, passed communications down to civilian staff through lower-down governors or a full prison meeting. When the new governor first popped into the department, I thought I must have misheard who she was because of the easy manner with which she told us to 'pop down to her office if we wanted to talk'.

'That was her? The new number one? Are you sure?' we asked the managing chaplain, who confirmed that she was indeed. We shared smiles around the office at the thought of the changes she might usher in.

One of her first moves was to insist that the prison residents were called by their first names. No more 'SAUNDERS!' shouted up the corridor, but rather Maz, or Gloria. This was not, after all, the military.

The second, more controversial, move was to replace the word 'prisoners' with the word 'residents' in our daily announcements and meetings. So the Tannoy would announce tinnily, 'All residents to the dining hall' rather than 'all prisoners'. We should not, she reasoned, assign 'prisoner' to people as their central identity. They may live here, but they're also mothers, women, trans men, people, hairdressers, solicitors, etc., and it did not benefit anyone that this should be replaced by a daily labelling as prisoner.

It was a measure that received mixed reviews from the staff and residents alike, ranging from 'We've gone fucking soft' and 'If I'm a resident can I just pick up and go then? It's not a bloody Travelodge', to gratefulness for the small dignity it bestowed, or complete indifference that it had happened at all. I wondered whether it might be sugar-coating the situation slightly, but I did think it made a cultural difference at least and took the sting out of those occasions when a frustrated officer would use 'prisoner' as a word to demean or put down. Spitting, 'Because I say so, prison resident' doesn't have the same menace in it; it's rather more factual.

I was pulled up on one occasion because I said, 'The girls were wondering . . .' and the number one responded, 'I think we should call them women, don't you?' I was never so pleased to have been reprimanded.

Her arrival was also marked by an increased recognition of International Women's Day. It had been in the calendar the previous year, but I couldn't remember much about it except for a dreary notice-board display and one of our multiple annual poetry and poster competitions.

This new governor, however, marked it by painting the chipped white gates throughout the jail in suffragette green and purple. I felt quite tearful when I first saw them being painted by the works team. The reminder of history's struggle for women's liberation also jollied me along to expect more for the women of HMP every time I opened and shut the gates.

In an effort to increase knowledge of women's history for International Women's Day, the activities department organised a visit from a local museum. They brought artefacts from the suffragette movement – banners, pamphlets and sashes in purple and green – documenting the journey of those women. It was a popular session and names had been put down some weeks before. Unfortunately, there was a miscommunication about timings so the group had been moved into the classroom two hours before the historians were due to arrive. I was summoned from next door where we were screening *Made in Dagenham* as part of a session on the gender pay gap.

Yasmin, head of learning and skills, gave me a pleading look. 'Mim, I don't suppose you could help me out – I've got a group for two hours with nothing to do before the historians get here. You couldn't run something, could you?'

I'd actually been looking forward to a morning watching a film, but Yasmin was one of my favourite staff members, so I left *Dagenham* with the sewing sisters staff and went to join the session next door where 20 women sat around four large tables.

'Right everyone, we've got a little delay until the museum guys arrive so we're going to start by going round in a circle telling each other which women inspire us and why.'

There was a collective groan and someone put their hand up. 'I thought we were going to learn about voting?'

'We definitely are,' I replied, 'but just not quite yet.'

I could probably have dredged up enough facts about the fight for suffrage to cover the first ten minutes, but in truth I couldn't quite remember which Pankhurst sister did what exactly and did not want to be the purveyor of fake news. I asked one of the officers if he could go next door to kindly print off the results from a Google search of inspiring women.

'I'll go first,' I said in the meantime. 'Do you know who Rosa Parks is?' A couple of people nodded.

'She refused to give up her seat to a white man, and it led to a bus boycott and helped end segregation,' someone offered.

'Exactly. Anyone else got an example?' I was met with silence.

The officer re-entered with a sheaf of papers with pictures and bios of Anne Frank, Frida Kahlo, Paula Radcliffe, Amelia Earhart, Marie Curie, etc., their faces etched with thin discoloured lines because the printer in the adjoining office was running out of ink.

We scattered them around the tables and everyone spent the next few minutes reading profiles of courage and achievement in the hope of finding inspiration.

'Right, from my left, who's got an example of someone inspiring? It can be one of these or someone else.'

The woman to my left was fairly quiet and picked the skin from her right thumb as she spoke. 'My mum,' she said. 'I've been a pain in the arse for her. Bringing trouble to her door, but she'll never give up on me.'

It was a story that provoked nods of recognition.

We moved along the line. 'My mam,' said the next woman. I knew she had grown up with the familiar knock of social services at the door, and so was surprised that she too could think of no one she was more inspired by. She continued: 'She could have got rid of me. That's what they were telling her to do, and she had her own issues she was dealing with. She tried her best, even when she had her own mental health problems, she tried her best to do right by us.' Again the group nodded.

We had Victoria Beckham after that, and then another line of mums. Someone read from the sheet about Anne Frank and we were back, once again, to celebrating mums.

We got to the end of the line.

'Shall we write to our mums,' I suggested, 'until the museum comes?' I thought of my mum, who I'd forgotten to phone that week. 'Tell them what you've been telling the rest of the group. Or if you'd rather not,' I added, thinking of those who wouldn't have one to write to, 'you can write a letter to your younger self, or maybe a daughter?'

The group nodded. Half because they were, by this time, so bored of listening to odes about 20 people's mums that they were glad of another task, and half because in that pause before the suffragettes, they had remembered the women to whom they owed life, no matter how flawed that gift of life or its delivery had turned out to be. I wrote to my wonderful flawed mum too, on pink folded classroom card with a felt pen floral border.

The museum people eventually arrived, wearing period costume and armed with boxes of wonderful artefacts, which they began to set out in a line across the row of cream-topped tables.

By this time, though, *Made in Dagenham* had finished and I was called to resume the gender pay class, where I planned to hold a debate on whether the issues from the film still affected us today. 'I don't think we get it worse at all,' Phoebe started us off before I'd managed to go through the format of a debate. She swept the rest of the group with a glance that said, 'Go on, you just try to disagree.'

She was fairly new in the jail and had been transferred from a large city. She wore diamanté sliders that were the envy of the wing and had her hair pulled into a slick ponytail on the top of her head and fixed with a hairband that looked like a bow. She hadn't been in one of my classes yet but I had already heard of her from the women who were. She had arrived with perfectly manicured nails which had prompted a mixture of admiration, jealousy and irritation from the other residents. But she was bold, creative and stood up for herself, dancing on the line without actually crossing it. She spun a strand of her hair around her thumb as she spoke. 'We get doors opened, bought presents, we got everything we need to get what we want right here.' She ran her hand down the length of her body and winked. 'You can't do that if you're a man.'

Like many of the women inside, Phoebe was 'on the game' – although unlike many of the other women, she didn't do it to support her drug habit, or anyone else's. It was a career choice. Rather than having to rely on a pimp, she marketed herself online and chose her own prices and clients. Despite her rhetoric, her work had greatly benefited from the fact that the internet had brought about greater agency for sex workers by providing a platform to self-advertise.

It was quite a good starting point for a discussion on the gender pay gap. Before I'd met anyone on the game,

I'd assumed that it must be quite good in terms of pay per hour. Even those with a pimp surely enjoyed a 60:40 split? This, I'm afraid, is wishful thinking. The majority of women I've spoken to over the years are what's called 'survival sex workers', who are in the game because they haven't got a lot of other choices. There are plenty more women like Phoebe, but without drugs or partners on drugs, they're less likely to end up in jail, meeting me. The women I meet are getting more like 10 per cent, or even being paid in drugs and housing rather than cash. The almost universally male pimps often have a group of women in their employ and rake in the takings in return for protection, not from them, incidentally, but from other people. In other words, it's a racket. Survival sex work has a worse gender pay gap than almost any other industry. It makes the Ford factory in *Made in Dagenham* look like the staff team at the *Ellen DeGeneres Show*.

'All right then,' I continued, 'does anyone disagree with Phoebe? Anyone think that women get a raw deal in any other way?'

The group looked around, waiting to see if someone else would break the silence.

'Why don't I give you a few examples? Seventy per cent of domestic homicide cases are female – that's female partners being killed as a result of domestic violence. Women are more likely to be victims of sexual assault and get harsher first-time sentences. Women in Hollywood are paid less and have to take their clothes off more.'

There was another brief silence until Lesley piped up: 'I don't see anyone's boyfriends having to go out on the game.' Lesley was always the first to offer to wash the brushes after the day's painting session. She had dyed red hair and her face showed the signs of being worn over the years by heroin use: hollowed-out cheeks and yellowed teeth.

Phoebe rolled her eyes. 'No one's making you, babe. And no one is setting your prices that low either.' She skimmed her eyes up and down Lesley's body, and planted her arm exaggeratedly on her hip. 'I enjoy my job, and my clients look after me well in here – private cash, trainers . . .' She counted the benefits off on her fingers as she listed them.

I started to sense that there must have been some argument from the wing going on here that I was not aware of, and the spat was worming its way into our discussion in the guise of a price war.

'Okay,' I said, trying to divert the conversation away from an impending fight. 'What about media coverage? What do we see women pictured doing in films and newspapers?'

By this time, though, I'd lost the group. Some people nodded vaguely but most stayed looking at

Lesley to see how she would respond to Phoebe's challenge.

'Erm . . . and what about the red rings on celebrities' bodies in women's mags,' I continued, to little response. 'Do they take as many pictures of blokes with cellulite?'

'Just leave it,' Lesley then said to Phoebe. 'It doesn't even involve you.'

Phoebe continued, getting increasingly agitated as she did. 'The thing is, babe, it's you making the pay gap, because your prices from the kerb are rock bottom so you drive down the prices for the rest of us.'

'Phoebe!' I interjected. 'One more word and you're going on a bully book.' My debate, it seemed, had failed to convey the sisterly solidarity of the feminist cause. Even as I spoke the two rose from their seats and started towards each other, Phoebe accusing Lesley of bad-mouthing her on the wing.

'We do the same thing,' Lesley shouted, 'don't you go thinking you're better than me!'

It was not the International Women's Day I'd had planned. But, like the purple and green gates which asked the question: 'What does it mean for us to be equal?', it was worth a go. And perhaps female empowerment in the prison didn't look and sound like the feminism that I knew, or would even be called feminism, but it probably didn't have to. Instead, it took the form of slow-growing confidence in one's ability or pride in a new qualification, or a decision to walk away from a toxic relationship, or in the celebration of your mum. Things had not gone quite the way I'd imagined – a slickly run 60 minutes of female solidarity and empowerment – but as the new governor settled in and we talked more about how to empower the residents, alongside how to keep order, I realised that my structured pay-gap debate had not been what the prison was missing after all.

DECK THE HALLS

Each morning would begin with a wing briefing in the education staffroom, where the duty manager, Kathy, would update us on the previous night's goings-on. The idea being that before the groups of residents arrived, the rest of us would be prepared for the fallout from any incidents that might have happened overnight.

The reports ranged from the mundane to the tragic: two listeners were called to B wing during the night; a suspicious smell, suspected to be Buscopan, reported on I wing; Rachel Jones is thought to be selling prescription medication: keep vigilant.

Occasionally the briefing was studded with more interesting nuggets, always delivered with dry humour by Kathy, her short-back-and-sides crop and flowery Zara shirts completed by raised eyebrows.

'Okay. Wiiiiing J. Some double A batteries were found

to have been stored in Francine Smith's undercarriage for an unconfirmed amount of time. Flipping 'eck, it's bad enough licking a battery – I've done that before – but having them down your knickers isn't going to be good for you. Francine's in maths this morning so whoever's on maths today expect a fully charged lesson. Wahey!

'And on C and B wings, Georgie Johnson was punched in the dining hall by Hannah Mitchell. The incident was said to follow a disagreement over pushing in in the dinner queue. To be fair, Georgie, no one likes a queue jumper – we're British.'

Kathy's bright deliveries would always make for light relief after the occasional sombre news that a resident had been 'blue-lighted out' to hospital after an overdose or suicide attempt.

The report then ended with the usual office reminders: 'Could all staff using the milk please replace the milk, and could whoever borrowed Cassie's Disney Princess mug please return it. If you haven't got a specific mug, try to use the NOVUS conference mugs.'

After the briefing, we passed round sheets listing those on self-harm or suicide watch – the ACCT list – so we could keep an eye on them in our classes and report on their mood in the bright orange folders that accompanied their movements. Watch levels ranged from four observations an hour to one a morning, with comments like: '10.00: Sarah seemed down and reluctant to participate'; '12.45: Maggie initiated conversation; when asked how she was feeling she responded "all right today thanks".'

As we neared Christmas there was a small but steady increase in the number of ACCT documents that appeared on the list. It was, depressingly, as much a part of the festive routine as the shredded tampon snow that lined pad windows as decoration. The dip in mood resulted from a catalogue of factors: a heightened awareness of absent families, a reduction in the activities schedule as staff took Christmas leave, the recurrence of painful memories of Christmas past and the ubiquitous power the festive season has to shine a light on our emotional dysfunction the country over. But, as with everything, the festive-emotional-dysfunction phenomenon was magnified by the quite literal storm-in-a-teacup effect of the enclosed prison environment. A reduction in sandwich size, temporary gym closure and arguments over frequency of bedding change can assume life-affecting proportions when you can't take yourself off for a walk and a latte and realise you're probably overreacting.

Everyone tried to do their bit. Because staff were stretched, some of the governors missed their own family Christmases to stay on and help fight the fires, as a display of support. And for our own part, to try to help counter the annual Christmas tradition of self-destruction and bleach-tablet smoking, our creative efforts intensified – and the cleaning cupboard was locked.

(You may be interested to know that smoking bleach tablets does not actually get you high. It is, however, rumoured to produce a false negative on a mandatory drugs test (MDT) if you want to conceal the fact that you've sniffed the heroin replacement Subutex. After a Kinder Egg shipment of 'subbies' followed by rumours of a spate of MDTs, the receiving wing might suddenly decide to have a spring clean. But the first Christmas I worked in the prison, there was a little wave of unrelated bleach smoking on the wing reports. I guess some people just got restless and smoked what was on hand.)

The new governor, though, had brought in changes. To counter the prison's mood, she introduced an activities programme as a helpful distraction. The prison choir endlessly sang carols, whole-prison bingo ran in the dining room where lucky winners would return with shower gel and tinned fruit salad, and people deemed 'at risk of decline' were moved into our classroom to keep their minds and hands occupied.

Our team (of two) gladly accepted our role in the production of festive fun / distraction. It was finally time for our glitter and harmonies – sometimes the subject of sarcastic remarks by other prison staff – to receive the appreciation they deserved. The new governor's approach was a welcome change from previous years when decorations had been heavily policed. Last year the A and B wing Christmas tree was, within a week, replaced with a gaffer-taped tree outline on the lino floor, making the main corridor look like an alpine murder scene. It was accompanied by a note saying, 'You can have your tree back when you've learnt not to steal the decorations', and remained into the New Year. This time round, however, Christmas was back on. An inter-wing decoration competition was called. B wing became white with cotton-wool snow, E wing transformed an upturned table into a sleigh, and A wing taped a life-size paper fireplace we'd made in the classroom over the breeze block corridor walls.

Alice and I had offered to collaboratively write and perform a pantomime. As a result of emptying the 'at-risk individuals' off the wings and into purposeful activity, my group for the start of the project predictably arrived accompanied by a large stack of purple and orange folders. The orange ones are the aforementioned ACCT documents. The purple ones the aforementioned 'bully books'. In general, the larger your stack of purple and orange, the tougher the crowd.

The group were, underneath a thin veneer of bravado, universally nervous. In stark contrast to my Stagecoach childhood, a number of them, due to school exclusion, care system involvement and unsettled home situations, had had short theatrical careers. Performances of *Oklahoma!* in homemade gingham dresses, as it turns out, are not in the essential section of the hierarchy of childhood needs. And yet, in all my am-dram years, I had rarely seen such brilliant creativity: skits of the ugly sisters appearing on *The Jeremy Kyle Show*, and Snow White battling addiction – the gang of dwarves and their captive young woman taking on a more sinister tone when seen through the lens of the group's all-too-shared experience. The group was a well of creativity, possessing a huge amount of real-life experience of what were, for me, only fictional themes. But they often struggled to find the words to say what they meant and even more to write them down. Instead, I printed sheets of paper listing emotions and characteristics for us to assign to the characters: frustrated, overwhelmed, intrigued, earnest, delighted – and we tossed them around, scratched out, circled and compiled them. We chose photos, drew mind maps and pictures and improvised themes. I collected the results and wrote them into the script for *Snow White and the Seven Co-accused*.

It was set in prison where Snow White was a bad girl come good, who was so named because she used to be a cocaine dealer and addict before her rehabilitation – aided by her offender supervisor, Officer Charming. Her seven co-accused began the play with an improvised montage of them walking across the stage. There was:

Buscy: who had a rather unfortunate Buscopan habit. She walked into the curtains and hallucinated invisible characters as she passed through.

Debty: who owed out her canteen package to everyone on the landing before it even arrived. She looked pleadingly at the audience while showing them her empty pockets.

Subby: a Subutex user who ground up lines on the chapel lectern.

Grass: the confidante of Governor Evil, who followed the governor everywhere.

Officer No-Keys: the generic name for a prison resident who likes to boss other residents around.

Pad-thief: who spent the duration of the performance trying imaginary door handles to see what she could pinch out of imaginary pads.

The observant among you will notice that this is actually only six dwarves. After some up-and-down weeks, our cast thinned slightly, and even with the staff playing a part (or two), we lost a dwarf. Plus, casting was not without its own issues. As we doled out the parts I asked one girl whether she'd rather play Grass or Pad-thief and she stormed out, shouting, 'I'm not a fucking grass, what are you trying to say about me?'

It is one thing feeling able to reveal a little of yourself within a group of eight people you've got to know, but quite another to expose your vulnerabilities and flaws to a wider audience of assorted work parties who had been invited to the performance. The fear that their fictional reputation would filter into a non-fictional reputation was keenly felt among the whole group. Hence, Grass and Pad-thief fell to me, and Officer No-Keys to Alice.

Jane was our Governor Evil. She had never been in a play before. Between the ages of four and 15 she'd chopped and changed among so many children's homes and foster carers it had left little need for extra dramatics. After a morning of the group playing around with improv and sliding off topic, she glowered at the room and announced fiercely, 'I didn't get to be in any plays when I was a kid so I'm making up for it now; you lot had better not fuck this up for me.'

She was a phenomenal pantomime villain: teardrop tattoos offsetting the pencil skirt and tights we persuaded her into, borrowed from one of my housemates. During the rehearsals she kept going off script, adding impromptu rants about how Snow White was a disgusting little cunt, and scattering the text with additional 'fucks'. She remains one of my favourite people in the jail.

However, in the midst of our dramatic triumphs, we were having other problems. Our Snow White, Laima, was having a bad month. She had a bereavement which, after months of speaking about 'getting herself clean and right', left her winded and spiralling downwards.

When we started the project, Laima had been excited to get the part. She'd viewed the lead role as a helpful distraction from her depression. Upon being asked, she proudly tied a blue ribbon borrowed from the craft box around her hair. The following day she had worn a blue tracksuit to match the ribbon, an outfit that suited our jailhouse Snow White perfectly. But as the rehearsals went on, the black cloud that hung over her did not abate. Anxieties, along with the number of thin red scars along her wrists, grew. Until, a week before our performance, she was sadly taken out of the class.

'I can be Snow White if someone else is the narrator?' our class's peer mentor Penny offered when she heard the news. 'There's more of that ribbon in the cupboard and my pad-mate has a blue top I can wear.'

She had been busy painting offcuts of three-by-two timber black. They were left over from a DIY project I'd finished and I'd brought them in, along with some wooden lolly sticks, to be constructed into the radios that Governor Evil would use to communicate with the officers. She set aside the paint and went into the cupboard to dig out the blue ribbon.

Officer Charming, Hope, took Penny's offer as the cue to accept a promotion to narrator. 'I'd prefer having the lines written down anyway,' she said, picking up the doctored library book which contained the narrator's script.

Karen, who'd been playing Buscy, was shuffled over to replace Charming and Alice added Buscy to the collection of parts she was already playing. We began rehearsals in our new characters, Alice practising the increased frequency with which she would have to dash behind the curtain to pick up a jumper or moustache to distinguish between her various guises.

'We'll start from Act 2,' I said. 'Governor Evil enters from stage left looking at herself in the mirror.'

Governor Evil: You handsome beast, look at your sexy eyebrows. They are just the most gorgeous things I've seen.

'Wait, wait, wait, pause a second,' I cut in. 'Jane, great entrance and I like your improv but what's with the eyebrows line?'

Jane huffed, 'Well I can't exactly say I've got great tits – not when you've invited the governor, the cleaning party, the English class and the sewing sisters!'

'You don't need to talk about your tits or eyebrows,' I replied. 'Try a line we wrote about how you're the most beautiful woman in the world.'

'I can't do that – tits is funny, eyebrows is funny. "Beautiful" makes me sound like an up-my-own-arse cunt. I'm not going to call myself beautiful in front of all those people.' Jane looked almost squeamish.

'But that's what the character is,' I reasoned. 'She's really full of herself. It's Governor Evil who's saying it. Not you. Besides, it's definitely okay to say good things about yourself.'

This wasn't an unusual sentiment from Jane. Earlier that week I had found myself filling out her self-assessment sheets myself because she'd only completed the 'things I could improve on' section and had left the 'things I am good at' section blank.

'Let's work on it later,' I said, 'when the others have moved on to prop making. Right everyone, why don't we go back to the first scene and practise the entrance again. So that's everyone off stage except the narrator.'

The characters collected on the other side of the plastic chairs that signified the stage's wings, leaving just the narrator on 'stage'. Her cardboard fairy wings hung slightly unevenly, so it gave the impression that she had been involved in a scuffle. The outfit was completed by a red feather boa which shed its feathers across the tiles of carpet floor as she circulated.

Narrator: I'm here to tell you about our hero,
She is beautiful and bruised.
And here she comes! Snow White
With her seven co-accused.

The characters filed on as their names were called and completed their catwalks, sashaying from the left-hand chairs towards the opposite pair which served as 'stage right'.

Officer No-Keys mimed blowing kisses at the officers who would be sitting in the front row, and, as practised in our method-acting exercise, Buscy hallucinated her way across the stage.

Narrator: But even with her cheery gang
        It's not all dance and song.
        For they were filled with terror,
        When Governor Evil comes along.

Jane entered the stage with her three-by-two radio.

Governor Evil: Governor Evil to MR77 [she spoke into the painted wooden device, mimicking the radio communication which echoed around the prison]. Who's the fairest of them all?

    Off-stage mirror-radio: MR77 to Governor Evil. You are.

Governor Evil erupted into villainous laughter to end the scene, which caused an officer patrolling the corridor to look through the window in case we were having an emergency.

'Absolutely fantastic,' I told the group at the end of rehearsal. Because it was.

And rather than deny the compliment, as she usually did, Jane responded, 'Yeah. That's right. We're fucking fantastic.'

For the dress rehearsal we moved into the chapel to practise the play in the venue where it would be set. The chapel was always preferable as a location for our classes because it was the only place where you were permitted to break for a coffee. With the exception of when the hospitality class were being observed running a mock café in the education department, hot-drinks breaks were strictly banned.

Even as we met the group on the main corridor, I could tell our newly promoted narrator was not having a good day. Maybe it was the pressure of the upcoming performance, or perhaps it was something completely unrelated. Whatever it was, it surged up in the form of generally directed hostility. She refused to read her part and sat glaring at the group.

Jane sat down next to her, trying to comfort her. 'Hope, you've been such a mint narrator,' she said, and then in the same empathetic tone, 'and if you don't get the fuck on with it, it's not going to happen.'

It was unclear whether the words were a compliment or a threat. Either way, Hope responded by sighing, picking up the library book into which her script was stuck and rolling her eyes. As she waited for her cue for the first line she ground her jaw and moved it up and down as though she were chewing gum. Gum is a restricted substance so she was probably just chewing her own tongue, but, either way, the effect of it was to make her look completely bored with the whole thing.

She breathed out heavily before she started, 'Welcome to our merry clan, on Snow White's special day . . .' She looked as though she'd been interrupted from a good TV programme.

'Come on,' Jane interrupted. 'We're all going to look like twats if you say it like that.'

The comment was what Hope needed to throw down the book and then upturn a flipchart that the drug treatment group had left in one corner. We called an officer to collect her and added an IEP warning to her file. I heard later that she'd had some bad family news that morning and I suspected she was looking for a way to go back to the wing and be alone to process it.

Nevertheless, the whole incident had left us with one day to go and a distinctly dwindling cast. 'Could we have one dwarf?' I wondered. An Edinburgh Fringe-style one-man-seven-dwarves piece? A little avant-garde for a chapel panto perhaps.

We had half an hour left until movement so I called a tea break. While the residents were pouring coffee from the urns, Alice pulled me aside, looking worried. 'Shall we just call it off? We don't want to embarrass everyone in front of all the work parties. There's no way we'll make it work.'

'I really want it to go ahead,' I pleaded. I was partly thinking of Jane and partly about the overtime I'd put into the production. 'Even if it's just a few monologues rather than the whole thing. Let's wait and see how to-morrow's rehearsal goes. If the group really don't want to do it, we can call it off then?'

'If they do it and feel stupid in front of everyone then it's not exactly going to be a confidence boost,' Alice retorted.

We asked the group over coffee what they wanted to do. I thought that they would lose their nerve and call it off. A few people wavered, wondering about whether they'd look stupid performing in front of the other work parties, but Jane was the deciding voice.

'No fucking way,' she said, 'have I put on a pencil skirt for nothing. The thing is, people will only laugh if we act like fannies about it and go, "Oh no! I'm going to hide in the background because I'm embarrassed." If you give it your fucking best, no one is going to be laughing, they'll be thinking, *I wish I was fucking brave enough to do that.*'

Her speech said everything it needed to: that if you believed in yourself, everyone else would just have to agree and believe in you too. 'And if they do laugh,' she continued, 'I'll fucking kill 'em.'

The day of the performance arrived. I had brought with me, just in case, an amended version of the play to be read through by our cast of five in lieu of a full performance.

I was surprised to meet Hope on the main corridor. 'Sorry about yesterday,' she said. 'I actually wanna do it. Anyway you haven't got a narrator and I couldn't leave you in the shit. Also, Karen's ill.' Karen, our replacement Officer Charming, had been struck down by a bug that had been working its way around the prison for a week.

It was the end of our discussion about the incident, which would keep Hope on 'basic' for another week, and we walked over to the chapel with the rest of the chameleon cast quite peaceably.

The route to the chapel involves two locked gates three metres apart. As you must lock the gate behind you before proceeding to unlock the one in front, the journey to the chapel meant that our class had to squash up into the gap to let the whole group in before I locked the first gate and weaved through to the second. It always reminded me of the announcement on the London tube for passengers to 'move down inside the carriage'. My impression of the tinny voice asking everyone to move down the compartment was lost on the mostly northern cast, but it was always a funny moment: us packed in together, everyone jostling and laughing in the gate-cavity while they waited for me to unlock the second door.

When we got inside the chapel, however, we were greeted by a line of yoga mats placed side by side across our stage and a group from I wing limbering up.

'We're supposed to be practising our play?' I said it as though it was a question when what I had meant was a statement.

'Well, you can't have booked it,' the instructor replied. 'We've had this in the diary for weeks.'

'So have we,' I announced, reaching for the chapel diary. I turned to the day's page to demonstrate our right to the space but across the top was listed in biro: '8–10am: I Wing Yoga', with, underneath, '10am: Creative Industries Panto'. Paper-clipped next to it was the invitation I'd given to the chaplains.

'Oh, all right,' I relented. 'We'll go back to the classroom. I'll call a patrol.'

Because we'd been listed as being in the chapel on the morning's movement boards and movement was, by then, finished, we had to wait until the count was right before we could move back. In the hiatus, I found myself explaining about our panto to a sympathetic I wing officer, Rose, who helped to run the yoga class – about our lack of an Officer Charming, the imminent performance and now our reduced rehearsal space.

'RIGHT,' she said, turning to the yoga group after I'd finished. 'Who wants to skip yoga and be in a panto?'

'I'll do it,' the woman on the mat nearest to me replied. She shrugged, rolled up her mat and stuck her hand out for me to shake. 'I'm Zanne.'

'You'll be fine with Zanne,' the officer replied. 'She did the wing production last year and was brilliant.'

We made our way back to the classroom with our extra cast member in tow and an hour left until our scheduled performance. Zanne speed-read her lines and had almost totally memorised the script in a mere half an hour ('I listen to the radio a lot and I'm good at song lyrics,' she explained). There was a slight issue in that she didn't know where they came, though, so we agreed I'd nod at her as a cue.

The practice took a little longer than planned but as the work parties would only be called over when we requested them to be escorted to the chapel, it did not leave the audience sitting in wait.

'What about the number one?' Jane asked. 'I thought you'd invited her?'

Bugger.

Back in the chapel, I found the number one already there, inspecting the pink-glittered HMP sign propped up against the lectern ready for our performance.

'I'm so sorry,' I started, 'we're not quite ready.'

I hoped that she could not see the group assembled

in the other room, where Rachel was pretending to do a striptease with the feather boa from the narrator's costume.

'Don't worry at all,' she responded. 'I've got a meeting now so I won't be able to stay, but I'm sure I'll hear all about it later.'

It was rather a relief, in truth. I didn't know her well at that point and wasn't sure if she'd appreciate the artistic direction we'd gone for with Governor Evil, or all the 'cunts' that Jane managed to keep dropping in.

We were, against all odds, ready for the performance an hour later, after an in-situ run-through in the chapel once the yoga class had finished. We even decorated the chapel for the performance. Blu Tacked to each side of the door where the audience came in were two pieces of mirrored card, cut into ovals and backed onto a glittered cardboard frame, and a poster announcing the panto's title. Along with the sewing sisters and BICS class who we'd invited came a couple of groups from the other education classes and a few extra through-the-gate staff. 'We couldn't just bring one group,' the English teacher said apologetically, 'everyone really wanted to come.'

Behind the curtain that made up the wings, our group was feeling nervous. They jostled about the small space, making the curtain bulge out in places as it was moved by elbows and shoulders. 'There's so many people!' Penny said, looking panicked.

'It's going to be fucking fine,' Jane said loudly – although the way she rapidly moved her fingers, tapping out the finale song on the wooden lectern she was leaning against, made it seem as though the statement was meant as much to persuade herself as it was to galvanise the group.

It went without a hitch in the end, Alice and I circulating the stage back to the wings to come on again seconds later from the opposite entrance with a different hat. Governor Evil praised her sexy face with as much enthusiasm as I'd ever seen. Officer Charming remembered all her lines, even when I forgot the cues. Snow White skipped about the stage in blue ribbon. The narrator shed red feathers from her boa across the stage as she moved about.

The final scene, before the epilogue, was between Officer Charming and Snow White. After revealing their love and banishing the evil governor who had meant to poison Snow White by infecting her canteen, they hugged. Snow White then turned to Officer Charming.

'You saved my life,' she said, 'and I don't even know your first name.'

Officer Charming looked a little embarrassed before announcing, 'Er, it's Prince. An odd name I know. My parents were obsessed with "Purple Rain".'

Zanne's final line prompted the rest of the cast to

appear on stage and begin a rendition of Prince's 'Kiss': 'You don't have to be rich to be my girl . . .'

The audience joined in the singing as the cast looped arms around one another's shoulders. Hope loudly hushed the singing audience so she could deliver her final lines.

Narrator: After seeing that Snow White could do it,
Her friends knew they could too,
And with the right support now,
They gave up the sniff and blues.

They lived happily ever after
A house for our Snow White!
They had the seven round for tea
And lived a quiet life.

As she delivered the final line, she threw down the book and immediately came out of character, giving an exaggerated sigh to demonstrate her relief at the play's conclusion. The sewing sisters, BICS cleaning group, through-the-gate staff and education class cheered and stamped as the group collected again to bow. Jane joined in with the audience, cheering and punching the air, and turned to wink at me and Alice in the wings behind.

'Can we do it again next week then?' Jane said when

the audience had been escorted out, leaving us to clear up the props and have a debrief after the performance.

'You must be fucking joking,' Hope replied.

FACTS AND FIGURES

So I said I wouldn't hit you with numbers and now I'm sneaking some in. But I've included these – mostly from research by the wonderful charity Women in Prison – because it's a good point in the story to give a little more context.[13] And, also, because it's easy to pass off awful stories like Hannah's – who suffered unspeakable crimes when she was a child – as unusual, when, in fact, they're horribly common.

1. Women are held in 12 prisons across England. There's also one prison in Scotland, but none in Wales. If there isn't a women's prison available,

---

[13] 'Key Facts', http://www.womeninprison.org.uk/research/key-facts.php (date accessed: 17/09/18).

female residents will be held in a unit within a men's prison or Young Offender Institution (YOI).

2. Women account for about 5 per cent of the UK prison population. About the same percentage of women who are CEOs of Fortune 500 companies.[14]

3. 53 per cent of women in prison report having experienced emotional, physical or sexual abuse during childhood.

4. 84 per cent of sentenced women are there for non-violent crimes.

5. 26 per cent of the prison population are from minority ethnic backgrounds (these groups make up 13 per cent of the UK population). Black men, in particular, are 26 per cent more likely than white men to be remanded in custody. And they are 60 per cent more likely to plead not guilty.[15]

6. 70 per cent of sentenced women entering prison in 2016 were serving six months or less. (Enough to lose a tenancy, and have children taken into care, but not really enough time to make significant progress

---

[14] 'List of Women CEOs of Fortune 500 companies, https://en.wikipedia.org/wiki/List_of_women_CEOs_of_Fortune_500_companies (date accessed: 27/09/18).

[15] 'Research on Race', http://www.prisonreformtrust.org.uk/WhatWeDo/ProjectsResearch/Race (date accessed: 27/09/18).

around drug rehabilitation, trauma counselling or education.)

7. There were 12 self-inflicted deaths in women's prisons in 2016.

8. 48 per cent of women in prison have committed an offence in order to support the drug use of someone else.

9. Only 9 per cent of children whose mothers are in prison are cared for by their fathers in their mothers' absence. I couldn't find any data on how many women are looking after children while the father is in jail, but I'm guessing it's more than 9 per cent.

10. One Home Office study showed that for 85 per cent of mothers, prison was the first time they had been separated from their children for any significant length of time. A fifth of them are lone parents.

11. A prisons inspectorate survey found that 38 per cent of women in prison did not have accommodation arranged on release.

12. 48 per cent of women are reconvicted within one year of leaving prison. This rises to 61 per cent for sentences of less than 12 months. In other words, if we're wanting prison to break a cycle of crime, then it's not working.

13. Foreign nationals make up 11 per cent of the women's prison population. Some of these women

are known to have been coerced or trafficked into offending.

14. 46 per cent of women in prison report having attempted suicide at some point in their lifetime. This is twice the rate of men (21 per cent) and more than seven times higher than the general population.

GLOSSARY 4

CIVVY Civilian/non-officer staff like me who haven't had officer training: teachers, admin, work-party instructors, etc. If you've a civvy you're not supposed to get involved in any conflicts or security issues. You just write an IR (see below) or press a bell and wait for someone more qualified to come to your rescue or tell you what to do.

GRASSING Residents giving information to staff about other residents; the kind of thing that might lead to a pad-spin (see below). Staff and residents will universally agree that it's a terrible thing to grass, but also everybody's at it. It's difficult to spend a whole morning in a classroom and not know that Marcia has been passing drugs to Charlotte, or that Carrie wants to smack Jenny in the face as soon as she gets back to the wing.

IR This stands for 'intelligence report'. Every time I heard a piece of information about something bad that had happened or might be about to happen, I was duty-bound to report it. As a rule, I wouldn't file one about hidden craft materials, but I would for anything to do with drugs, fighting or bullying. It might be that someone was expecting a drugs pass on a visit, that someone was going to go back to the wing to punch their pad-mate, or that someone was being picked on. I would enter on the 'intelligence sharing' computer programme what I'd heard and who from, and then pick a risk level and threat category from a drop-down menu. The menu included the category 'threat of dirty protest', which I always wondered if I'd have to use. (A dirty protest is when someone uses either not washing or body-fluid smearing as an act of protest. Famously invented by the IRA imprisoned in Long Kesh in the 1970s.) The reports then made their way to a central office, where the snippets were pieced together to form a picture of what was going on – like something from a Second World War espionage film.

PAD-SPIN Aka a targeted room search. If there's been intelligence that a resident is holding or supplying drugs, or stolen items, etc., then they'll get one of these. Everyone hates pad-spins because the inspecting officers take all your carefully arranged cards and pictures off your pad's notice board to check behind them (a fairly common hiding place for contraband). Sometimes people give false information to provoke a pad-spin on someone they don't like. This generates widespread speculation about who provided the info.

PROP CARD/PROPERTY CARD. A card that details everything a resident owns in the prison. They're allowed an allocated number of tops, pyjamas, trousers, etc. Underwear is unlimited. If you want a new item from the catalogue (you can order some bits from the Argos or Avon catalogues), you have to put something back in your 'prop box', the in-prison self-storage system. If you are caught wearing something not 'on your prop', then you're usually put on 'basic' because you've either pinched it or traded it.

SECONDMENT

Our prison's few hundred residents would have fitted into just two of the ten wings which made up the men's privately run mega-prison that I'd been seconded to for two weeks to facilitate the writing and production of a collaborative book of creative writing and poetry.

It had a high turnover of residents and an industrial feel, vast stacked landings, frequently changing officers and front gates like ePassport control, except they scanned your fingerprint and ID to allow you entry through its automatic barriers. While at the women's prison I had come to know every pad and most of the staff, even after two weeks at the men's prison I couldn't name and locate all the wings, such was the scale of the place.

The prison's reputation had not escaped me. A series of online videos showed drug-fuelled pad parties and, like many other men's prisons, online comments were thrown around about how prisons were too much like holiday camps: a barbed-wire Butlins. Vague similarities to its Skegness counterpart included the fact that it had a farm site, a large-scale education department and a gym. And that, after my small, closed-movement prison, it felt relatively freer for the unescorted half-mile walk between buildings. That is, however, where the similarities ended – unless on my childhood trips to Butlins I'd missed the part where a happy camper could get their ear chopped off with a razor blade over a Spice debt. Of course, there were proper fights at the women's jail, but this place, in contrast, made it look like a peace camp.

There weren't enough jobs or training programmes for all of the residents so the bang-up was relentless. Hyperactive minds bricked for 20 hours at a time in a two-by-two cell, bordered by other two-by-two cells holding cooped-up and pissed-off men. These living arrangements meant that the prison buzzed with the tension of a shaken-up can of Coke. As though, always, a fight had just finished or one was about to start.

Such a vast perimeter coupled with a thinned-out workforce to patrol it also meant the place was riddled with drugs, and in particular Spice – a synthetic cannabis which has much worse effects than its humble soil-grown relative.

I'd been given a tour a few weeks before I started when

I'd come for introductory security talks. The prison was split into 'two sides'. The smaller side was dubbed 'the dark side' – this was not how they introduced it on the tour, of course, but something I learnt quickly during my time there. It was where residents were put for their own protection if their crime, temperament or associations meant that they would have been a target in the 'main jail' – this was the other, larger side. Each side had its own education department, library and dining room and the two were separated by a long path and a series of gates. In between lay the geriatric wing and drug treatment unit: the prison's in-house old people's home and rehab.

As we were led round the estate, we were greeted at the doors of the geriatric unit by a man leaning on a Zimmer frame and talking loudly to himself. Another old man, slumped in an armchair and holding the same regulation blue plastic mug of tea that we had in the women's prison, shouted in reply, 'Frank, would you shut up!' He turned to us and explained in a thick Somerset accent, 'He's like this all day – not a bloody moment of peace and quiet.'

As if prompted, Frank resumed his slightly incomprehensible shouting and, as he did so, spat the top row of his false teeth onto the plastic non-slip floor in front of him. The man in the chair creased up laughing and caused himself a coughing fit, which made him spill his tea down his regulation blue jeans. The residents of this jail, unlike ours, were dressed identically apart from their shoes. One of the slightly younger residents helped to mop him up with blue paper towels from a roll.

Visit to the geriatric unit complete, the officer took us back out of the gate and onto the pathway to resume the tour. As he locked the gate he raised his eyebrows and said, 'He's considered a very dangerous man, that Frank. He'll never be allowed out.' I thought of his wrinkled hands reaching for the saliva-covered plastic teeth on the floor and wondered what he had done to spend his twilight years inside.

Our tour took us away from the two living quarters towards the workplaces. Along the path was a warehouse for the laundry, which must have washed thousands of sheets and towels each month. It pumped the synthetic cotton smell of fabric conditioner into its adjoining courtyard along with fabric fibres from the dryers, which settled to look as if the path was covered in snow.

On the same row, an industrial recycling unit housed cardboard balers and stacks of crushed one-metre cubes of plastic waste. Men in high-vis vests sorted bin bags into piles, and one waved at the officer as he passed. 'Morning, sir!' The officer returned his wave. 'Keep up the good work, Scott.' His familiarity brought me back a little to the prison experience I knew better.

At the end of the path was a surreal farm comprised of locked fields, one of which was home to about 30 gated goats. Several of them were standing on top of an old wooden picnic bench which looked like it had been added to the otherwise empty enclosure to give the goats a viewpoint. Alongside them were chickens and then vast polytunnels growing potatoes, cucumbers and courgettes (which, I was assured, were actually used in the prison kitchen).

We passed an aviary, which, the officer explained, used to house a flock of canaries. It was now empty.

'We had to get rid of them,' the officer explained. 'Someone tried to pass drugs by shoving them up the birds. We couldn't have that. For one thing, we'd have had the RSPCA over.' Every time I passed the unremarkable wired box during that fortnight I was reminded of the anus-stuffing which led to the demise of the prison's ornithology efforts.

It was all quite surreal, I thought: like a mad gated village. A different world to the one I knew.

The plan was to run creative writing sessions in the main jail in the mornings and over on the 'dark side' in the afternoons. That way our collaborative book would be written without its contributing authors ever having to meet.

The main jail where we started was populated with

men mostly in their twenties and thirties. After the tight regime of the women's prison, where residents were signed in and out rigidly, I was shocked to find that my group arrived in dribs and drabs as the vast prison moved the different wings one at a time, taking an hour to collect a full class.

Not unusually, I was quite quickly fond of the group. The men were kind, funny and very committed, although they espoused a rather unique brand of respect. During the first session a beefy tattooed man called Ant berated the rest of the group for swearing in front of me. 'Never in front of a lady,' he said, his biceps adorned with a pin-up tattoo of an out-of-proportion lingerie-clad woman.

Because of the lack of jobs in the men's jail compared to the women's prison, the residents were also much more enthusiastic about activities and, crucially, had all chosen to be there – sending in apps to the education department some weeks before, when the course was advertised. It made a welcome change from the frequency with which new-starts to the women's prison programme greeted us with: 'Creative industries? Well I'm not fucking doing that!' Or: 'I'm going to say I've come on my period so they have to send me back.' Instead, the men even used the notebooks we provided to scribble stories over lunch hours and evenings as well as during class time, and then each day we had a feedback session.

'I've written a story about going lamping,' David, one of the men in the class, began in one of our first sessions. The story, written in strings of dialogue, described David and his brother's haphazard teenage efforts, hunting rabbits with dogs and lights:

Facking ell John, git your dog back, he's ripped the facking fing t pieces.

Nah, man. He laaavs it.

We're spost-ta bring the rabbits back. We'll not get paid if you cannae even tell what it were.

Let im ave one, ya twat . . . etc.

It was quite like Irvine Welsh's *Trainspotting* in its quick, witty dialogue, written out phonetically in cockney dialect. He hadn't read *Trainspotting*, though, and had written the story not as a mimicked literary technique, but as an overflow of his thoughts and experience.

Ant told his story next. It described, in depth, a complex diamond heist with holes dug, safes opened and a spontaneous murder of a disloyal friend.

'Really great plot,' I complimented him after he'd finished. 'You had the captivating beginning, the drama in the middle, and a good ending, just like we've been talking about.'

'Is it?' Ant replied, chuffed by the news. 'That's actually just how it happened.'

Bugger. 'The story is about you?' I asked tentatively. We were discouraged from dwelling on people's crimes in case it appeared we were celebrating them.

'Oh yeah. I thought you said we could do it about ourselves or make it up?' Ant said, looking surprised at my own surprise.

The other tutor attending gave me a small head shake and we moved the conversation swiftly on. And so it continued, a fortnight's worth of raw, vulnerable, accidentally autobiographical writing. Prose centred on violence, guilt, abuse, death and drug-taking, often running in page-long sentences without speech marks, commas or full stops. The range of experiences in the place meant that there was little need for imaginary drama.

In a prison which – even more than in the women's, it seemed to me – took kindness for weakness, their vulnerability, like Lilly's, was a hard and courageously given gift to our class. The excitement about being published, even anonymously, in our in-house ring-bound A4 book, put together by the business admin class, motivated them.

Their kindness, though, was not a sort I had encountered before. It was expressed in courtesy and hard work, but also in a protective and very normalised violence towards anyone they suspected of being disrespectful. The days were peppered with shows of strength – played out in dialogue but ready to prove itself at any moment. The presence of this violence, along with ubiquitous drug-taking, was casually threaded through our conversations and almost every piece of creative writing. An offhand threat about razor blades followed by a carefully written ode to a beloved son on the outside. Bloody noses, Spice-induced psychosis or ribs broken in punishment for rude remarks about a family member barely turned any heads.

This currency of violence was marked by visible battle scars on the residents' heads and arms – apparently from blades, baseball bats and screwdrivers. Some of them, the men bluntly relayed, had been inflicted by rarely present fathers or uncles. One man, in his twenties, showed me the red impression left by a removed tattoo that stretched from one side of his back to the other. 'It was supposed to be a picture of the game *Snake*,' he said. 'You know? Where the snake is chasing the dots and gets longer when you eat them – it was on them Nokia phones. When I was 12, my dad and his mate put it on me with a tattoo gun when they were drunk. A teacher saw at school and social services paid for it to be removed.'

It struck me that in women's prison, pain, anger and frustration were visible more often through networks of thin white scars and raw fresh cuts along their own bodies, whereas in the men's prison it seemed to be expressed by scars and cuts inflicted on the bodies of others. It did not surprise me also to meet those who were inside because of violence inflicted on women. They were the other side of the story that we so often heard in the women's prison.

After a week of seeing and hearing and reading, my head hummed with the bravado and brutality of it. I took a handful of stale biscuits from the staffroom office and walked the half-mile to the goat enclosure for a little distraction. The goats climbed and clambered over the picnic bench. Their enclosure was constructed using the same high metal fences as bordered the prison and they were locked in with the same wide metal gate as closed onto the wings. As I unlocked the enclosure the group of animals ran over to me. Just a few at first, until their momentum brought the herd into a swirl around me. I locked the gate behind me quickly – out of habit and to avoid escapees – and carried on towards the picnic bench, the circle of goats following.

They gratefully took the biscuits I came with and then stayed, squabbling around me and nibbling my clothes and hair. A large male placed his front legs on the bench where I was sitting and leant over to catch in his mouth the plastic prison ID card that hung on a lanyard around my neck. Their warm breathy bodies tripping over one another for week-old rich teas was remarkably redemptive. It is hard to ruminate on tales of trauma and violence when you are confronted by something as immediate as a rough-haired billy nuzzling in the pockets of your department-branded black jacket for extra hidden carbs.

And so, after Ant boasted of losing his virginity to an adult babysitter when he was ten, I visited the goats. And again when Mike, another student, explained that, because he got a – now banned – IPP (Inside for the Protection of the Public) sentence when he was a teen-ager, his 14-month tariff still had him locked up seven years later as there weren't enough staff to review it. The goats' heady smell displacing the contents of my saturated brain. It's a weird thing being overwhelmed by the sadness of a situation that you're only really on the sidelines of. It's a circle of finding it all a bit much, and then feeling guilty for that because you actually live quite a nice life, and then finding it all a bit much again.

My afternoons on the dark side provided an eerily calm contrast. The slightly odd mix of people who'd been separated for their own protection made for a surprisingly peaceful workplace, albeit with a sinister under-tone. The violence of the main jail was veiled on the dark side and sprouted up through a surface of courtesy mostly in the form of more subtle manipulation.

We began each session with an introductory round for everyone to share without interruption or challenge.

Brian volunteered to start us off. He explained that he had put his name down for the sessions some weeks before and had been looking forward to it. He was thin and pale with a pudding-bowl cut. He read the *Beano* and battered copies of Agatha Christie novels. And, as asked but rarely heeded, he had brought with him several copies as an example.

Halfway through the afternoon he beckoned me over and handed me a composition that he'd been working on in anticipation of the classes. The main character was a little girl who was abducted by the devil from a shopping centre changing room. It was, in its paragraph-long description of the little girl's agonised expression, an awkward read. The description itself was actually quite good but, for good reason, along with talk of one's crimes and explicit sexual activity, children's stories were not appropriate writing fodder on the dark side.

Brian watched my face as I read to observe my reaction to his unfolding plot. 'Brian,' I started. He looked up expectantly. 'Fantastic use of adjectives.' His face lit up. 'But this is much too dark for our project. For one, satanic abduction is quite a heavy topic; it's a bit much for in here. And, I'm afraid, you can't really have any child characters at all. It might be that horror isn't really going to work. I'd like you to try a different genre. What about some descriptive work about the wing in here?

Or even a fable, like "The Hare and the Tortoise", if you want to stay away from realistic writing.' It felt a bit nanny state, admittedly, but was part of life teaching in a prison.

He went from looking crestfallen to thoughtful, and then gathered up his loose sheets of lined A4 paper and said, 'Thanks, miss, I'll have another go now, in my pad.'

'Keep up the adjectives!' I shouted as he hurried out, tucking in his shirt tail as he went.

It was the sort of conversation I hated, but he took it surprisingly well, I thought, being told that we didn't trust him enough to include any under-18s in his stories, unless they were rabbits.

(I made a mental note to check whether underage rabbits were permissible.)

Gradually the group finished their pieces. Steven read out his poem about his daughters in an ABCB rhyming structure. Then there was Michael, who brought us a rewrite of *Animal Farm*. It was set in the prison and I suspect written using animals because it allowed him to make criticisms of people that would otherwise have resulted in him being told to fuck off by the other inmates. He began the story with clucking hens who gossiped in the laundry, making nests of the white fluff. He wrote about the red-bottomed gorillas from the main jail, beating their chests in the gym and making themselves heard with shows of aggression and shouts, and about the tortoises moving slowly about the geriatric wing. He and his friends seemed to remain conspicuously absent from the menagerie.

Towards the end of the week Brian decided he was ready to share, placing the now typed-up sheets he'd copied out during his IT lesson down on the side of my desk with a nod. His new composition was a sci-fi piece and contained a brilliantly constructed world. Well-developed, likeable characters, thoughtful introduction, playful and light. It was hard to believe it was written by the same person.

'Was this all you?' I asked. 'It's such a different style.'

He nodded to the name at the bottom of the page. It read 'Kitty'.

'Oh, sorry, I thought it was your new piece. Is this one of your examples? I've not heard of Kitty.' I asked, thinking his story must be still unfinished.

He pointed towards himself and whispered. 'It's me, I'm Kitty. Actually,' he started, looking sheepish, 'there are three of us.' He stared out of the window, narrowing his eyes, and a moment later said, 'But it's mostly just me and Kitty. We don't speak to the third one. Malcolm is why we're in here. Fucking Malcolm.'

'Oh right,' I responded inadequately. 'Gosh.'

I'd known people with multiple personality disorder

before, who felt like a host of characters jostled for attention in their head, but this seemed a little different. Brian's three personas were more deliberate, with each character permitting him to express different parts of himself.

I suppose there are parts of me that I'd rather didn't exist. I can be mean and oversensitive and judgemental. I'd quite like it if I could point to those thoughts and words afterwards and blame them on my alter ego Fran, or drink three-quarters of a bottle of Merlot and say it was Penny. And, of course, there are parts of me that are too bad to even write down – if I could call them fucking Robert and cut them out of the conversation rather than confront them then, at times, there's no doubt I would.

As I got up to leave on my last day, my head was swimming. It was a different beast, the run-for-profit men's prison. Its scant officers had left the de facto rule of the place to the loudest, the richest, the biggest and the readiest to fight. It had almost reminded me of *Lord of the Flies*.

But my head wasn't swimming from that; it was *actually* swimming. It must be the long commute, I thought, and the heavy days. I scanned out for the last time and made my way to the car. But as I sat down and couldn't quite see straight, I realised that it must have been the

Spice fumes that odourlessly filled the corridors around the education toilets and regularly sent other staff members into dizzy spells and fits and comas.

I sat in the car park waiting for it to pass and for my vision to realign, and felt glad to be going back.

THREE POEMS BY GEMMA

LIVING HOMELESS

Wake up unwanted, unloved and dirty.

See a rat in the street that gets more respect than her.

No self-respect when you have to be flirty.

Everyone looks.

And no one will touch.

All the students judging her by what they've read in books.

The Sanctuary is a place where she can get food and a shower.

A tough life on the streets, you live minute by minute, not hour by hour.

All I own is a sleeping bag and a crumpled-up photo,

Taking heroin to make her warm.

A security guard kicked her in the head, telling her it's
time to go.

All I want is to die.
Wishing the next crime she commits will take her back
to prison.
Why won't anyone help her?
All I can do is wonder why.
A young girl with a beautiful heart.

She's an angel that no one can see.
For the dogs down there just rip her apart.
She'll soon be another statistic.
Why would anyone help her.
They believe all they hear about the streets.
It's all mystic.

MY DEMON

It's so black and dark.
It wants everything you have.
But you still light the spark because it's the only thing
that loves you.
And makes you feel warm and soft.
But yet, it's killed most of the friends you know.
And it's killing you too, slowly every day.

So why do I love it so?
Because it makes the pain go away.
But it won't let anyone else love you.
'I'm sorry . . .' And 'I won't . . .' – that's what it makes
    you say.
I pray every day that I'll walk away.
Please God, hear my prayer.

This Demon has a hold of me
And all eyes look to see that shame it makes me feel.
It hurts my heart.
It's not just killing it, it rips it apart.
I love you so much Lord but it knocks my faith.
You make me sleep on cardboard.

Even when the good Lord helps you win the war,
And you walk with your head high,
Instead of dragging on the floor.
You're like a cancer patient in remission.
Always scared it comes back,
That's the devil you call addiction.

PRISON

The walls are dirty and white.
I'm here because I did wrong, always thought I was right

The door locks and I feel so alone.
But after a while this hell starts to feel like my home.

At first this place is the thing I hate,
Yet I feel so understood, with all my girls I can relate
Down the hall I hear a scream, then the reality hits me.

I never realised women could be so mean.
She will play and manipulate you
You'll be sorry if you come in and you ain't got a clue.

A kind word will go a long way
All of us are in the same boat
Short or long you're here to stay.

Be quick on your feet, use your head
The dining hall isn't just where you eat
Business gets done and deals get made.
You'll be sorry if you've made them wait.
Sugar and water or a cut to the throat.
A life taking, but in hell they'll be waiting.

Take the good with the bad
Stand your ground
Make it clear you're not going to be had.
Look around and see, it's not all dodgy deals and bad
    looks.

Then I start to feel that this is the place for me
My heart's turning cold.
All I can do is reject
Another lost soul stuck for life
A victim to the system.
'It's okay,' she says. 'At least I have my life.'

It's not okay. There's more to life than bars and keys
Fuck prison morals and respect.
You need to realise all you need in life is a bit of
    SELF-RESPECT.
Now I'm free.
No more bars but prison still left me covered in scars.
In my recovery, the only one who counts is me.
All the friends and relationships are now just a memory.
Prison is a fake world.

SEASIDE IN THE SEG

A plan to brighten up the slightly dreary segregation unit had been in the pipeline for months; it had been one of the recommendations from an inspection sometime before in response to some worries about poor mental health over there. Someone had even bought a selection of paints in different blues ready for the task. They had, however, been sitting in the segregation unit's cleaning cupboard ever since, waiting for someone to use them.

'I don't suppose you could take on the CSU mural?' Ivy asked one day when I went to hand in my week's job preference forms. Ivy was straightforward and ran the allocations department, which placed residents in jobs and training programmes. She wore a trouser suit and her hair in a low ponytail. If she had people she was finding it hard to place, she'd put them with us for a while, so we were regulars at her office, feeding back and making new plans for people moving on. She probably received more flak than anyone else in the jail because staff were rarely happy with who they'd been allocated and made sure she knew. But because she was slightly outside the day-to-day workings of the wings, she'd also managed to avoid the prison staff cabin fever, so the stress had not succeeded in dulling her creativity or appetite for new ideas. I always enjoyed popping into Ivy's office once a week to talk about plans for art competitions and poetry exhibitions. Ivy continued: 'We planned a seascape mural ages ago but the person who was going to do it moved departments, and we've had the paint sitting there for months.'

The weather was sunny at this point and I could think of little better than to paint the courtyard of the unit over the summer's afternoons. It also fit neatly into the prison's new enabling environment initiative which we'd been called to a meeting about the previous week. The idea was that we'd find ways to give the residents more ownership over their spaces, greater responsibility and to empower them to improve the prison's association rooms or to start community groups.

I was relieved not to have to order in the paints. What could be allowed into prison was a bit of a minefield – water-based paints were allowed, oil-based banned, plastic pots preferable to metal etc. Painting projects I had initiated before had never got off the ground because of not knowing who could authorise them, or rather who would want to.

'It would be a long-term thing,' she went on. 'I could allocate one group to do a block of sessions to paint the background and then over the year different people could come down and paint fish and plants on it, and it would gradually grow with different contributions from different people. Like a community mural.'

It was a brilliant idea and saved me having to come up with a new project for the summer season. Because it would have to be a small group and the project did not require anyone to sit down for extended periods of time or be confined to a small space, it was also perfect for people who, like myself, were attention-deficit and found themselves itchy and irritable in a classroom environment.

The following day I visited the works department to borrow brushes, rollers and disposable painting suits, and a few weeks later we had four people signed up to paint the first coat of an ombré blue which graduated in depth as it moved along the wall that boxed in the CSU courtyard.

It was the most therapeutic session I had ever run. The meditative action of paint-rolling repetitively on a white wall as the colour crept around the circumference of our block was almost mesmerising.

'This is the most relaxed I've been since coming in,'

Adele claimed as she cut in around the edges, dripping blobs of blue onto the concrete floor as she did so. 'I don't even mind that I've ruined my shoes.' She gestured down to her white Nike trainers, which were now decorated with spatters of blue in the two shades, matching the concrete floor.

'I can't believe how quiet it is! You don't even feel like you're in jail,' Danielle added.

I didn't think Danielle would come, so I was really pleased that she'd made it. These inclusion sessions weren't mandatory, and her social anxiety meant she struggled to attend regular groups – so it was a nice surprise to see her waiting at the pick-up point almost as soon as movement began. 'I'm just going to try it,' she said on arrival, as though to lower my expectations in case she found it all too much.

She was right about the strange isolated calm. While the CSU was meant to isolate drugs or drama, when it was empty it also kept out the frenetic energy which filled the rest of the jail. For the afternoon it was our little blue oasis.

Once we'd covered the first side of the three courtyard walls we were painting, we broke for water. As we drank, sitting on the concrete steps, we rolled up the legs of our crêpe-paper suits to catch some light from the sun, which had broken through clouds to bleach the courtyard. Adele interrupted our silent sunbathing by joking about our head-to-toe paper suits and pretending to keep finding clues on a crime scene investigation or to be completing a biohazard clear-up.

The painting had been faster than we'd anticipated so we stretched out our water break to fill the time. All of the women were set to be released in the coming months, and so we talked about the seascape legacy that would be here long after they were gone.

'One month. Then I'm going to be out of here,' Grace said. 'Never to see this sea again. I'm going to get rid of all the clothes I've worn in here and get a new set, right down to socks and knickers. Then I'm going to go straight over to get a salt beef bagel from the shop right at the top of Brick Lane, the first one you come to. With gherkins.' Grace was one of our London migrants, whose East End accent made me nostalgic for the places, tastes and sounds that had made up my own childhood.

'I just want to see my mum and kids,' Adele said.

'I can't wait to see my donkey, Wobble,' Danielle chimed in.

'Your what?!' Grace replied, incredulous.

'My donkey,' Danielle confirmed. 'I've had him for years. I used to take him around with me or just go and hang out with him on the grass.' Danielle grew up in a Welsh coastal town where the small estates were bordered with grassy fields, and donkeys and horses were apparently tethered to posts. 'My auntie is looking after him now, but only a few months till I get to see him again.'

Her explanation was met with a moment's silence and then Grace, usually quite shy, suddenly screamed with laughter and bent double, rocking on the concrete step where she sat. It was the kind of explosion into laughter that caused us all to jump as though shocked. Between laughs she managed to get out, 'Maaaaate! . . . a donkey called Wobble! . . . I thought you were going to say proper food, or sex or your friends! . . . Faaaam . . . not a donkey.'

Her yelps of laughter dissolved into silent, rocking giggles which spread back to me, Danielle and Adele, who laughed too until, with wet eyes and aching stomachs, the hilarity petered out.

'I just really fucking love that donkey,' Danielle said, starting everyone off again as we washed the brushes in the small sink in the toilet once we'd completed the blue background that would be the canvas for our picture.

The next week, we planned to return to add some fish to the as yet empty sea.

'We definitely get to paint the first fish,' Adele had insisted. 'We've earned it. And otherwise the next group won't know what to do.'

I agreed: only once the wall had its example fish

would it be ready to be populated with sea life by the prison at large.

But the morning before the fish-painting session, I got a phone call from allocations. 'I'm afraid there's been a fight and two people have been relocated down to the seg,' Ivy said. 'So we're going to have to cancel the session.'

'Could we not just do it anyway and make sure no one goes near the windows?' I asked.

'Not really,' she replied apologetically. 'It's created a bit of a drama and the officers are worried that they'll shout out of the window and your group will pass back messages and stir it up, or be pressured to bring something down to pass in to them.

'We can rearrange for next week?' she offered. 'I can't think they'll still be down there then.'

By this point it was too late to amend it on the activities register, and so during movement I stood at the locked seg door, relaying the news that we were postponed to the women as they arrived and sending them back to the wing for the afternoon.

'Oh whatttt!' Adele exclaimed. 'I've even remembered plastic bags to go over my trainers.' She held up a torn canteen bag and some hairbands from which she planned to construct makeshift shoe covers.

But the unscheduled free afternoon gave me a chance to do a bit of outreach. Anyone still on the wings during work hours was either a wing cleaner or unemployed, and so it was a good time to catch people who would benefit from being involved but did not have the confidence or motivation to fill out an app to apply.

There had already been talk of who would paint which sea-life version of themselves so I was met, as I walked up the wing corridors, with heads popping out of cell doors and other residents collecting in the passageway to put their names down. One of the women, who sported a collar of tattoos around her neck, greeted me with, 'Put me down, miss. I'm doing pufferfish 'cause I'm fuckin' spiky.' She raised her chin and folded her arms as she spoke. This prompted peals of laughter from the other women, a punch on the arm and a suggestion from her pad-mate that they do a joint contribution of kissing fish instead.

'You should do some crabs,' another woman said to her friend, ''cause you've definitely got them.'

'Put me down for a dolphin. Oh no, actually a mermaid.'

The officer hearing the commotion appeared to check that I was managing. 'It's for the mural,' I explained. He smiled at the suggestion that the excitement was prompted by a large painting rather than some juicy gossip about a drugs shipment and rounded the corner again back to his office.

By the time I had finished my round of three wings,

my list of painters had filled the available lines on the sign-up sheet I'd brought with me, the names invariably accompanied by suggestions of sea animals which were to appear on the walls.

My original group eventually met the next week to christen the wall with its first sea life. Danielle painted a large colourful fish, using almost every one of the tester pots of paint I'd found in the cupboard to depict scales along its back and a large fin which pointed straight up.

Adele had felt quite comfortable with the sea but did not quite feel up to painting a fish yet and so instead decorated the bottom edge of the design with seaweed. The painted vegetation disappeared into the grass and weeds coming up through the hairline cracks in the concrete floor, and so it rather wonderfully looked as if it had grown up through the gaps.

Grace painted a large red crab at head height

'Crabs don't just float in the middle of the sea, you idiot!' Adele commented when she saw it. 'They walk along the ground. That's why they have legs!'

'Oi,' Grace replied, 'it's supposed to be my imagination – the crab can go wherever she likes.' She then proceeded to paint a red smiley lipstick mouth on the crab in a bright scarlet, which clashed with the orange body and looked as though it was pouting at onlookers.

It received mixed reviews. 'It looks more like an

orange spider,' the officer in the seg commented afterwards. 'It's not that clear which ones are claws and
which are supposed to be legs so they all just look like
legs. And why is it floating in the air?' It was secretly my
favourite of the collection of sea life.

For weeks after that, either the CSU was populated or
I was busy with a different event or activity. I arranged a
few more sessions but had to cancel them all when the
unit filled up in the days before.

Max kept catching me on the corridor. 'Any chance
of another couple of sessions on the wall? It looks
a bit weird with a few fish in a massive sea.' Max was
the bearded segregation unit officer, universally known
as one of the most helpful men in the jail. He was the
person I approached if I ever had to fill out a nicking
sheet (when you have to make a statement for the in-
house court system) or open an ACCT and couldn't
quite remember the training for how you did it.

'Sorry – I'm trying to get down!' I'd say. 'If you could
see if there's a way we could get in while other residents
are down there it would help the process along!'

'I'll see what I can do,' he'd reply.

True to his word, Max sorted out an exemption if
there was only one occupant. However, this small step of
progress coincided with my summer holiday, so by the
time we booked the next session, a number of months
had passed since the crab, fish and seaweed had been

added (as well as one of those toothy deepwater fish with a light attached to its head, painted by our intern).

But, happily, once I was back from my holiday the unit was empty so I popped over to Ivy's again to schedule in another session with the names I'd collected from the wing. I handed her the list of names. 'I've just checked and there's no one down the block at the moment so hopefully we'll still be clear on Thursday. Just put in a group from the list.'

Ivy's job was like a rather complicated game of social Tetris. She had to find combinations of people who would not come into conflict with one another or be at risk of between-wing passing, and who hadn't been involved in the same crime. Looking back, it reminds me of constructing the table plan for my wedding – making sure there was significant enough space between UKIP-supporting second cousin Trevor and our friends who are refugees from Syria, while not compromising the separation of the outspoken vegans from the even more outspoken fox hunters.

Ivy looked surprised at my request and then a little awkward. 'Has no one spoken to you?' she asked.

'About what?' I replied, suddenly worried that perhaps I hadn't counted the brushes back properly and one had been found on the wing.

'The number one was in the seg and wasn't thrilled about the mural. He's going to have it painted over.'

She looked reluctant to have relayed the information. 'I don't know if it might have been that crab? Or it looked a bit messy with only a few fish?'

The mural project got started while we still had the first governor I worked under, and I didn't know him well enough to ring up and find out what the problem was, or whether it had just been an offhand comment about the crab which someone had taken a little too seriously.

'Isn't he leaving soon?' I replied. 'Surely it'll all take a while to get organised?'

'I think they want to do it as a summer project while people are away so there's a few more job places for people off work. I'm surprised no one has spoken to you, but it seems the ball's already rolling. I'm sure they did try but . . . you were away,' Ivy said apologetically.

'Did you explain about it being a community mural, and that more fish were coming when I got back?' I asked.

'I did, but it wasn't the number one who spoke to me, just someone seeing whether we had a spare painting group. I did tell them to speak to you about it.'

I was stunned and livid in equal measure. 'The women have spent hours on it. Does he know we only just did it and we're coming back to it? Does he know what it's about, who did it or what went into it? This is bullshit.'

I got a call a few days later from the officer who'd

been tasked by the number one with the mural's removal. 'Scott here. I'm ringing because I hear you're the woman I need to talk to about arranging a painting group?' he said, clearly unaware that he was hitting on a sore point. 'I've got to get a group together to paint over the CSU, and Ivy says you're the woman to talk to.'

'Not to get it painted over, I'm not!' I replied. 'We've only just done it! Can I not just get another group to add some more fish?'

'Ah, I'm afraid not,' he replied, sounding more apologetic as he went on. 'Paint's already been ordered and people aren't sure about the fish anyway, you see. Something about it being a punishment unit not a playground? It's funny,' he continued, 'we've all become quite attached to that weird little spider crab now. He's a freaky little feature of the place. We'll be sad to see him go.'

He paused, as though my reassembling the painting group to cover up their work was still on the cards.

'Scott,' I said, mustering my courage, 'the project was part of the empowerment initiative. You're asking me to get my group of painters, who've already designed and painted a painting on the wall, to paint over it because someone or other didn't like it and the paint's already been bought. That's not very empowering.'

'Right,' he said, 'I see. I'll have a think who else I can ask.'

He set the phone down and I went to find Alice to rant.

By the next week the officer had seconded a group from one of the in-house training programmes.

Even a drugs incident that resulted in two people being relocated to the unit was not the saving grace that I predicted. It seemed that the 'no painting while the segregation unit was in use' rule did not apply to other people.

I never did go down to the unit after that to see what our mural got replaced by. I also never told Adele, Danielle or Grace what became of their segregation sea-side legacy. I knew the number one would not announce the paint-over to the prison population so it was unlikely they'd find out. They were all to be released in a few weeks anyway. Adele back to her kids, Danielle back to Wobble the donkey and Grace back to the bagel shop at the top end of Brick Lane, to order a salt beef bagel with gherkins.

NOTES FROM A
COUNSELLING JOURNAL

Today Alison and I talked about 'escape thoughts' at counselling. You know, the ones where you think, just for a moment, *If I accidentally walked in front of this train right now I'd have a good reason not to go into work tomorrow*, or, *All I'd have to do is swing my steering wheel 180 degrees and whoops: off the side of the cliff*. And then your brain feels shocked by the appearance of the thought, as though it was dropped in by someone else rather than having constructed itself in your own head.

I thought about not telling her about them in case, what with that and the low moods and constant bugs and colds, it meant I was suicidal. Except, you know, only for random periods of seven or eight seconds several times a day. The stupid thing is that I only didn't want to tell her in case she stopped me going to work.

They reflect, she said, your brain trying to process that you're not in a great place, but instead of rationalising a route out, or changing the things you fear, it conjures up these brief extreme escape plans. The irony is that I'm the only one that's not trapped – I can swipe out and leave. Somehow, cracking up under those circumstances feels a little self-indulgent. I know it shouldn't, that's what we always talk about, but it does.

If I rationalise it, there's not one good reason for not wanting to go into the prison. The minor incidents – a little aggression, a few threats – that tipped me over into feeling melancholy were, I know, empty. I liked Charis, I felt I understood her. I'd feel really fucking angry if I'd had her life too; besides, she's in the seg now and won't come back to the class for a while. If I rationalise it, I know that it wasn't even really about me; I was just the person in the way on a bad day.

Alison is trying to help me understand it as a cumulative effect. I might have felt more robust about Charis if it wasn't for the drip, drip of stress.

I suppose that's what you get if you take a group of women who struggle with their mental health and box them up. The box is too confined to hold all of the storms and rages. And you want to be part of the lifeboat team, coming in with your orange ring, but then all of a sudden you feel overwhelmed by it too, even just going into the box at all.

Even reading this back I think, *Mim, stop being a drama queen. You've got a lovely fucking life and should be grateful, so stop whining.*

I am still working on having fewer critical thoughts about myself but it's not going fantastically well.

I have not yet talked myself into wanting to go to work.

RABBIT?

From: Miriam Skinner
To: Rebecca Harris
Re: Therapeutic rabbit

Hi Rebecca,

I happened to notice that some dogs came in today
on behalf of Stray Aid and was just wondering what
the possibility was of getting the sign-off from security
to bring in my rabbit? He's house-trained and has had
experience working with adults with learning difficulties –
quite robust.

I think he'd be of therapeutic benefit; we could even
partner with mental health? Either way, let me know!

Thanks,
Mim

BLACKY

Blacky and I were sitting in a loading bay in front of the bus station in the 1998 bottle-green Golf I'd borrowed from my housemate. I was dropping her off after a group camping trip and we got talking about this book.

'I'll be in it,' she said. 'There's nothing about jail I don't know.' She proceeded to write a permission note on the back of a used envelope she found in the glove box, which I wondered whether the lawyer checking over the book would accept. I took a photo of her holding the envelope in the hope that it would strengthen the case.

I never worked with Blacky inside. I'd heard her name but she'd not been in for quite a few years and so we just missed each other. I'd been glad, though, that she was able to join our women's resettlement group on the outside for a camping trip. She was larger than life, had her hair almost shaved at the sides with patterns cut into it, and was great fun. She was the first to leap off the high rope swing at the forest camp to show us how it was done, and then cheered each person who attempted the swing, pushing them higher or slowing them down when they'd wanted to stop.

That morning she had woken with the shivers and shakes only an alcohol-dependent person can describe, and had consequently begun the day with some deep glugs of cider to allow her muscles the stillness they needed to get dressed and pack up the tent. It took her a few hours to warm up to being the Blacky we had known from the night before. In front of the rest of us, she drank it from a Ribena bottle topped up with black-currant squash. 'It's not fair on the others,' she told me. 'Some of them might be in recovery and I don't want to fuck it up for them just 'cause I need it.'

'Shall I start from the first time?' she said, making herself comfortable in the grey upholstered passenger seat. I nodded, showing her the recording button on my phone and tapping on the red circle to signal the beginning of the conversation.

'Right, the very first time I was scared. Well, I was 15. I had been locked up for burglary. I was in a children's home before that. A special school. Residential. School was my home if that makes sense? I lived there five days a week because I had learning difficulties, behavioural problems and mental health problems.'

She said all of this in a string, barely stopping for breath, as though listing a historical chronology rather than her life.

She continued, 'Or I might have been 14, I can't remember now. 13 or 14. So, anyway, the first time I went into prison. Back then you didn't go in a paddy wagon – you know what a paddy wagon is, don't you? The jail vans? Well, I didn't go in one of them. I don't know if it was because of my age or what, but I went in a police van. They took us from the courts to the jail with no other stops.

'I walked in and I shit myself. Don't forget, I'm only 15 years old but I've got this little bravado thing going on. You know? When I lived in a special school I had to front up. You know when you watch things on telly and that? Like *Wentworth*. Or it was *Prisoner: Cell Block H* back then. You see characters in that playing big, and you think you've got to put a bit of bravado on. Years and years ago, before I got there, my nickname used to be Munchkin. And now it's not. I've not been Munchkin for years. I put a front on and I'm still fucking wearing it now. I only drop it when I'm on my own with my dog.'

Blacky stopped the flow of words and turned to me to ask if she could open the window, before continuing.

'So I go in and I'm thinking, *I've got to give it all I've got. Can't take no shit, 'cause if I do, I'm going to get done in.* That's what I was thinking from what I saw and watched, so that's what I did. So I've gone in and given it all the "bad I am" and I remember this one screw. She was on reception at the time. I think she's a SO [security officer] now? Miss Slatcher, right? She was only young, 27 or something. But she was lovely. And I came in reception and just felt so much of a like, "you're home". It was because of that Miss Slatcher . . . I don't even know what she done. She smiled at me or whatever, I might have been crying or something, I can't remember exactly what it was. I might have been scared. I might have been kicking off pretending I was dead hard or something. But I can remember her looking at me and just saying, "Calm down, you're okay." I don't know what it was but I felt at home.

'And I don't know why I felt like "you're home", 'cause it's jail, right? How the fuck can I be at home. I'm 15 and in a jail.' Blacky laughed at the incredulity of it. 'I'd not had a home up until then. My stepdad used to do a lot of bad things to me, my brother and my mum – and make us watch too. I didn't have a home outside. The only time I could say I was at home was when I was living with my nanna. And I was only home on the weekend after I started the special school, and on the weekend I didn't want to see my stepdad so I was out with my friends burgling. I wasn't really home because I didn't belong. I didn't belong anywhere until I came in.'

Despite her blunt honesty, she delivered this assessment in the same resigned tone in which she had delivered her initial chronology and stated the way she took her coffee.

'So anyways. I've got on the wing. At the time it was men and women in the same jail. With me looking the way I do. You know . . . I'm a butch girl. Lasses who were in jail. And I'm really sorry for saying it blunt like this, but they either want to fuck ya or fight ya. Right? Not in a nasty way. Half the population wants to fuck ya, half the rest want to fight ya. But at least you've got a fuckin' place. I felt like I belonged. So then I got out – I was there for nine weeks the first time – I wanted to get back in. They put me on community service or something instead. But I remember this moment when I was sat with my mate in the snow and I thought, *What have I got out here?*

'And I was back in about five weeks later. By this time, I'm still 15 but I'm on drugs and that now. I was still a kid. All I wanted to do when I got back in was see Miss Slatcher but she wasn't on. I was on the YO wing and I gave a big impression. I was fighting all the time, getting nicked all the time. Never got done in, though. That's a good thing . . . it isn't really, but it was at the time, to not get done in. And it was like, I belong here. This is what home's like. The residential school was just a school. No one wants to live in a school. At home, no one wants to be abused – but there I was somebody.

'So for a lot, a lot of years I used to get myself locked up. It's hard to explain that. It sounds mad. You know when you go home and see your parents? Well that's how it felt when I came back in. How can I put it? I felt like loved inside because I felt safe, I felt secure and I felt that I was somebody. That doesn't even make sense. But if you close your eyes and imagine you've been to college and you're going home, when you walk in your mum and dad give you a cuddle. You go into your bedroom and you know where everything is because that's your house. That prison was my house.

'I saw Miss Slatcher every time I was in. Probably every single one of those screws I've been nicked for shouting at, but not Miss Slatcher. I've never, ever shouted at or disrespected that woman. She made me feel like I mattered. No, do you know what it is? She made me feel normal. She made me feel like, "you're not an outcast, you're not this, you're not that". When you're a kid and you go into a jail after living in a hostile situation and someone just says to you, "You're all right." You know? A little thing like that can make you feel okay. I'm not saying I loved the woman. I just respected the hell out of her. I was a cunt in there but I would never, never be disrespectful to her.'

Blacky ground to a halt. 'Right, that's the nice bits,' she said. 'What do you want to know next?'

'What about after?' I asked. 'When you left. Do you want to talk about when you got released?'

'Right,' Blacky said, folding her arms in her lap ready to give another account. 'I've got out of jail 18, 19 times with nowhere to go. You go to the council: "Nah, we can't help ya." Go to the social: "You've got to wait and go on Jobseeker's Allowance, you've gotta do this and do that." The fuck? That takes weeks. So where do you go then? There's nowhere to go other than to go back. To where you're safe and secure.

'So what you do is, you take that £98 – that's what you used to get if you had nowhere to go to on release – and you go begging or you go shoplifting or into prostitution, whatever it is you do to get by, then you buy a parcel – do you know what I mean by that?' She gave me a knowing look. 'Drugs. And you get packed up. And obviously, you know . . . you plug it.'

She widened her eyes and nodded. I returned her nod to show that I knew what she meant: put it up her vagina.

'And then you get yourself arrested and then you go in jail. Don't forget, you've already just been in jail so you're basically clean but you pretend you're not. You take a load of tablets before you go in that morning so they all come out in your piss test. You say you need sleeping tablets, you need this, you need that. And nine times out of ten you'll be on the gear already because you've just got out so you've gone for a buzz. So when you have a piss test all these things come up. You get given the meds and then you've got all them to sell too.

'Do you know what they used to say about me when I was going out? "Do you know what it is, Blacky, I'll see you next week, yeah? Probably Thursday." I'm being deadly serious. For a lot of years that's what I'd do. I'd get myself locked up for shoplifting, I'd go to the courts, and I'd say, "I don't have a bail address", even if I did, just so I could go back. If you've got no address it's automatically remand. That's how most women like me make their money – go out, get packed up, come back in, make their money, go back out.'

'You've been out a while now, though,' I replied. 'What made the difference? Did they find you a place to live?'

'Nah,' she said, shaking her head. 'I've never, ever, ever come out to a place. Oh, I'm lying. I have had help once. That's when I did my parole sentence. They got me into a hostel. But that's the only time I've got help leaving the jail. When I had the place I got clean and stayed out for six months. But the place they put me in was a doss-house. The house at the time was a derelict building for every smackhead, every crackhead, every alcoholic in Middlesbrough to go and get their head down.'

'So not like a rehab then?' I asked.

'I've never gone to jail and come out to a rehab, are you mad? I've never even got out of jail and got a proper B&B. That house was just 'cause I was on a parole sentence so they had to. If I went to jail now and got out in six months, please believe me, I'd probably be sat there on that pavement begging 'cause I'd have nowhere to go. It's fucking horrible to say it because I'm talking about my actual life. But when you go to jail, right, everyone says, "You get three meals a day, a roof over your head, secure." And it is like that, but it's not like that too. It's not the best thing for you. It doesn't really solve anything is what I mean. What if, instead, you put me in a nice B&B, or not even a nice one, just any B&B, right? Give me some help, somewhere to fucking belong, and maybe I might not go back and it would save thousands and thousands of pounds. Sending someone to jail does cost the government money, 'course it does. Doesn't it?'

'Any more things you want to know?' she asked, abruptly finishing the flow of sentences which struck me as a clearer proposal for prison reform than I had seen articulated in any *Guardian* article or online journal.

'That's great, thanks. It's really good stuff,' I replied, turning off the recording.

'Well, give me a ring if you need anything else. I'm always at home. You'll use my real name, right? Put Blacky at the bottom?' As she finished her sentence she was gathering together her belongings from where they lay in the footwell, having been rapidly packed up after our camping trip.

'I'll have to check if it's okay – I'm not really using people's names in case it accidentally identifies anyone else. But I'll ask, and if it's okay then I'll write "Blacky" at the bottom.'

I'm really glad I got to write it at the top.

BOURBON BANDITS

8.10am

Alice and I were sitting in the classroom listening to the trundle of movement. Mingled voices amplified into shouting which accompanied the patter of footsteps along the main corridor. The officer at our door left his post to rectify the commotion. Someone was escorted yelling back down the corridor. Vest tops, I thought, always vest tops. One of the residents sprinted into the classroom. As she arrived at the door she relayed the drama.

'Cherry's been caught with a packet of malted milks. They tried to take them off her. She kicked off and got sent back to the wing.'

It was illegal to carry off the wing anything other than your ID and your education file.

'One more thing, miss. When she got caught, she said, "But it's my turn to bring the snacks for creative industries! Ask Alice." I think you're going to get bollocked, miss.'

We were not allowed biscuits. The classroom had to feel like a workplace, and biscuit breaks were not a given in a workplace someone might have to go into on the outside. But we sneaked them in anyway, particularly on a Friday when the staff brought in biscuits for the staffroom – lots of the instructors did. Sometimes for a treat Alice would stop on the way to work and get a five-pack of supermarket bakery cookies, not available on the canteen, and cut the large chewy rounds in half for everyone to have a piece. Then we'd eat them away from the window in case we had a surprise inspection.

Cherry's inaccurate version of events wasn't ideal, I thought, but at the very most the consequence would be a raised eyebrow and the adding of weight to the general impression that we were pushovers.

We began the session as normal.

9.17am

The residents were counted and everyone accounted for. This means you're allowed to call a patrol and move from one area to another without messing up the figures. Cherry appeared almost immediately on one of these patrols, looking sheepish – and without biscuits – in the doorway of the classroom.

'I think I've got you in the shit,' Cherry said, by way of explanation.

'Yeah, I heard. Why did you say it was your turn anyway?' Alice asked. 'That makes it look like we're making everyone bring in biscuits.'

'I just thought of it on the spot,' Cherry said, smiling and resting an arm on the back of Alice's chair. Alice rolled her eyes.

'But they're not going to be that arsed about biscuits,' Cherry responded, laughing, 'not when they've got fanny-fulls of buscy to worry about.' She had a fair point.

10.09am

We were halfway through our first activity – learning to cross-stitch by sewing Tetris-block versions of our names on oversized cross-stitch templates. As biscuit-gate seemed to have come to nothing, Alice opened a packet of Bourbons we'd bought for the Friday tradition. Work was disrupted by the entrance of two black-clad security officers.

'Who's in charge here?' they said. Cherry choked on her Bourbon and covered the packet over with some spare leaves of A4 pastel-coloured card.

'Er, me,' Alice replied, blushing.

'Come with us, please,' the MI5 duo replied.

'Now?' Alice asked. 'We're halfway through the lesson.'

'Now,' they replied.

10.12am

'It better not be about fucking biscuits,' Cherry snorted.

10.19am

Alice returned, looking simultaneously a little ashen and on the edge of laughter.

'We won't be having any more biscuits,' she informed us.

The class erupted into whoops and cheers.

'They sent two SOs out over the fuckin' biscuits.'

'Watch out – it's the Bourbon bandits.'

'The sugar smugglers.'

'Gangsters of the Tesco cake aisle.'

'Shortcake pirates.'

'Rich tea trap-stars.'

This final suggestion was met with blank looks. 'Trap' is a piece of drug-related London slang that had not yet migrated into our northern lexicon.

'I think that's enough about the biscuits,' Alice interrupted, bringing the room back to relative quiet. 'Let's get back to cross-stitch.'

13.34pm

We were having lunch in the chapel.

'I nearly crapped myself,' Alice said, spooning couscous onto a plate for lunch. 'For them to take me away in the middle of a lesson in front of everyone – I thought it was going to be an emergency! One of them genuinely said, "Bringing in biscuits is as bad as smuggling in tobacco." I didn't know where to look!'

16.18pm

Walking along the corridor on the way to the education department, Lilly from our previous course stopped us.

'What's this I hear about the Bourbon bandits, then? Fucking biscuit legends.'

IMPERFECT HARMONIES

G wing was the closest thing you could get within the prison to a room upgrade. There was a list of the criteria you had to meet in order to get on the wing: being on consistently good behaviour, not smoking and not being on methadone or Subutex (heroin replacements) – only then could you put in an app requesting a transfer.

G wing, to use the tabloids' favourite inaccurate analogy, is the Center Parcs to the prison's Butlins. Although, in contrast to the free bike hire at Center Parcs, the main perk on G wing is that you have your own bedroom and the loo is in a separate room. While this might seem like a downgrade from the ensuite loos of the main jail, it actually means that you don't have to shit behind a curtain with your pad-mate within touching distance. That is, if your curtain is intact.

G wing residents are also typically older and less in

and out, which means the Kinder Egg deliveries of pills and powders rarely make it all the way there, so it's relatively drug-free. Any cross words, loo paper theft or cheeky fags can have you shipped back onto the main corridor within the day and back to communal crapping. This deterrent means that it's the most chilled wing in the jail, although, I'm told, still quite catty.

The wing itself is in a small compound with a path that runs along the front and side. While the wing is locked in, your bedroom door is not, so you can roam within this compound at any time before the 10pm curfew. A visit to G wing would often begin with encountering the short-distance speed walkers who liked to pace back and forth along the ten-metre courtyard, turning around a wooden picnic bench before coming back the opposite way.

On the second of two floors is a kitchen where the older women taught younger women how to make cheesecake using the sachets of coffee creamer you were given each week in a tea-pack and ingredients available on the canteen. In the association room next to the kitchen, several longer-termers would sit in the armchairs, sharing a coffee with the on-duty officer and knitting scarves to be given as presents to other women on the wing. The sight of them was both surreal and comforting. Knitting needles are, of course, banned. Instead, the scarves hung off sharpened pencils, the maximum width of the garment dictated by the length of the red prison pencils. The click-clacking of knitting needles was replaced by quiet wood-on-wood tapping as the long thin scarves appeared.

Although anyone could apply for G wing, it was renowned for housing the middle-class parking-fine fraudsters and embezzling solicitors. They tended to be the prison mentors and Open University students.

I got the impression that this group had never expected to be at the mercy of the justice system. They tended to be more surprised by it, more alert to the system's kinks and injustices. In a rather odd dynamic, residents in the main jail were far less shocked by the whole thing, though they had often been subject to much greater public and parental failing. Many had been funnelled in straight from homelessness, exploitation or the dreaded care system, and were more resigned to the situation having seen families and foster siblings go through the same routine. Although this divide was a source of tension between the groups, it was also a source of camaraderie. G-wingers were the people you asked if you needed help with your appeal.

I actually had little reason to be on G wing. Ours was inclusion work, and we sought out those who were on the edge of the system and struggling to engage. For most who attended our groups, high mental health needs and ongoing methadone use meant that G wing residency was unlikely, and, in many cases, unwanted. Even with the destination loo, G wing was not every- one's cup of tea – people worried about the strict rule- keeping and that you'd feel out of place or judged for being in drug recovery. It was well known for being cliquey. Other people found that after the clamour of the main jail, G wing was eerily quiet. The absence of other people's drama meant that a lot more time was spent in your own head, which might not always be a particularly hospitable place to be. I did, however, have a soft spot for the wing's residents. In part because – honestly – it was a bit of light relief sometimes from the drug-taking and trauma which populated the main jail. In addition to the pencil scarves, the wing was a hotbed of community craft, so they also more readily joined in with even my worst ideas – doily-making parties, panto- mimes and Christmas paper-chains.

But the choir hadn't meant to be a middle-class affair. It had been an offhand idea that I'd doodled into the schedule after a mood-lifting Capital Radio singalong to nineties band TLC in our classroom and a few episodes of Gareth Malone. I hadn't been in a choir since school and can't even read music, but loved the connection provided by singing together. I printed off the words to 'No Scrubs' and hoped we'd muddle along. It was, more accurately, mass-karaoke, with which I was better acquainted.

A week before the first session, I hung A4 sign-up sheets in the windows of each wing office. On the top they said in WordArt blue bubble writing: 'Can you belt like Beyoncé? Croon like Cheryl Cole? Sing like Sia? Then join our new choir!' The prison IT system was the only place I knew where I could still get WordArt and I found the fonts nostalgic. As a rule my on-wing posters tended to alternate between the rainbow-coloured arch of words and the blue one that thinned in the middle. That's the one I'd used on the choir poster.

Underneath the bold title there were two columns of dotted lines which ran down the sheet for names to be added. While we had respondents for every wing, G wing – bastions of extracurricular activity – returned a bulging list, including song suggestions. A few people had even written in brackets next to their names '(Alto!)' or '(can play piano)'.

In hindsight, this was what I should have expected: G wing made up the numbers on most of the prison clubs and socs. I was, however, a little disappointed. As fond as I was of the G wing residents, our projects were for the outliers for whom the choir should be a bridge to community. I thought perhaps I'd find that someone whose discovery of music would provide a route out of a cycle of addiction, a story which, of course, would then be made into a film and prompt a visit from Mr Malone. I was also hoping, with my lack of music theory, that the group wouldn't be that up on it either. And, more to the point, that they would already be familiar with the song for which I'd written an arrangement the previous night. I was now unsure if we'd be able to start off with 'No Scrubs' after all.

We met during afternoon association between dining hall and bang-up. It was after normal prison hours so I had to call the gate staff each week to let them know I was staying in. The few times I forgot resulted in those radioed hide-and-seek search requests ushering me to stand by a landline in case I'd got myself into hot water and no one had noticed my disappearance.

We were an eclectic bunch.

Joanne, who had a soulful voice, was in her forties and had chin-length dreadlocks that swung as she sang and swayed.

Pippa, who was a London transfer, could rap, had candy-floss-pink hair which reached down to her waist, and was someone I hoped would increase the choir's street cred.

Debs was an enthusiastic singer and local karaoke star with a drink problem.

Archer was a mum of three who had customised her Converse with pink glitter and embroidered butterflies.

Karen was in her sixties, plump, and immaculately dressed. She'd been in church choirs for years and was, crucially, endlessly patient with those who had never sung sober and needed a little encouragement.

Jade was a blonde Latvian who sang an ethereal soprano in both languages.

And Aly, who warned that she had a chronic health condition and couldn't commit to every week as it would flare up unexpectedly.

They joined our chosen soloists: Nihlani, whose hair was chopped an inch short all over and bleached blonde, paired with Jodie, who was a little shy but had enrolled on the Freedom Domestic Violence programme and was looking for opportunities to put her assertiveness techniques into action. While Nihlani and Jodie had never sung solo before, they earned themselves the roles by virtue of being the two who confidently knew the song. The chorus could be easily learnt by the remaining members.

We began each rehearsal by stretching and then dishing out singing parts (because the choir was hardly ever a consistent group this was necessarily repeated each time). We worked our way up a scale on the chapel piano and sat down on the line of pale blue chairs in the order in which we reached a register we could not hit, thereby assembling ourselves in a scale. Then there was always a warm-up folk song – needed both to re-engage the vocal chords and to get the group used to the idea of singing in front of other people.

In our first session, I introduced Nihlani and Jodie as the soloists.

'That's right,' Nihlani said, 'I'm the lead part. With Jodie, though, yeah? Not on my own.'

'Exactly,' I said, 'with Jodie.' As I spoke Jodie shuffled over from where she'd been standing among the sopranos to join Nihlani, as though needing her role to be reiterated before she felt bold enough to stand in the soloist's spot.

We started with the chorus as it was easier, and then Karen and I assigned different parts for the 'No'. The room filled with humming as people began to learn the tune and sing along.

It was quite beautiful, almost like it mismatched the context. The prison was full of singing – radio hits being shouted in unison by groups of women listening to Capital, Cher tunes escaping from the shower, or a half-heard rendition of Shania's 'Man! I Feel Like a Woman!' coming from the gym – but these tuneful, determined harmonies were a little different.

After a few practices of the parts, Nihlani and Jodie came in with 'I don't want your number'.

Jodie at first mouthed the words, but as the remaining members chorused 'NO!' in a beefy three-part harmony in response to her sung questions she began to produce sound too. At first it was barely indistinguishable from a whisper, and only audible when she accidentally began slightly before the cue, but before the end of the second chorus her thin but pitch-perfect voice could be heard throughout if you listened for it.

'No!' we shouted in chorus, we don't want your number, 'No!', we will not be pushed around, 'No!' The negative response echoed around the white-walled room and resounded off the Artex ceiling.

Archer was one of many people in for aiding and abetting a boyfriend who had turned out to be not so lovely after all. As she sang 'No!' in a top A, choosing to create her own harmony a third of a tone higher than the other sopranos, I saw her projecting it forward, her eyes glaring at a window at one end of the chapel.

No. They did not want any scrubs.

We took a break and I collected from the staff office my hidden box of Pukka Three Cinnamon to offer the group as an alternative to tea. Milk, I'd heard, was not good for the singing voice and the group was small enough for my stash to suffice. Their eyes lit up as I brought the teabags through. They weren't a product you could get on the canteen and the spiced steam that they released into the air was a smell of unallowed luxury. The teas led us to discuss tastes of home which had not made it through the gate.

'Ground coffee,' Karen admitted sheepishly.

'Sushi!' added Nihlani.

'Latvian food,' Jade said, swooning.

'Cheese,' Archer offered, 'not ready-sliced, ready-grated mild Cheddar from the dining hall, real cheese.'

'Yes! Brie!' Karen added.

As we drank the tea we leafed through the song books. We decided to move on from TLC and compiled a list including 'Lean on Me', 'Something Inside So Strong' and a selection of Christmas songs to be learnt for a few months' time.

The tea drinking and song selection had taken up the remainder of the session, so I called a patrol to escort everyone back to the wings before the evening's bang-up.

By the following rehearsal several weeks later I'd printed out the words for the additional songs. I also nipped into Sainsbury's over my lunch break and picked up some crackers and a small round of cheese. Staff were, I reasoned, allowed to offer biscuits within the confines of the chapel – and there was little practical difference in serving them with a few slices of cheese atop. Or with a bunch of grapes alongside them on the board. It was both a small dignity, the cheese, and meant that I could guiltlessly eat it as well.

And so it went: a block of Cheddar that second session, some Stilton during the third, and, by the time we had learnt Bill Withers' 'Lean on Me' to its conclusion, we were breaking with fresh blueberries, an actual cheese board and several types of cracker.

The cheese represented a change in direction for the choir. I had resigned myself to the fact that it belonged to all those who came and found refuge in it – even if it was mostly just G wing. It was their breathing space and, in an otherwise quite frantic week, it was mine. Where we could sit and talk about families and the week's activities, and the oddities of my job and how we could change the system and reform healthcare. The choir, unintentionally, had become the only place in the prison you could admit you missed avocado and be met with sympathy rather than an eye-roll.

Our hymn singing paired with cheese meant that we had also become a British cultural experience, and so the choir attracted several foreign national residents. We integrated their various languages into the songs. Rosie, a Korean woman, only knew English songs from the radio and, although she did not know the meaning of the words in Adele's 'Rolling in the Deep', requested it each week so she could join in with something. We continued to sing it in her memory after she'd been deported, missing her heavily accented rendition and the subsequent applause.

As we neared Christmas we tried to prepare a performance which would reflect every member of the group.

'"Pie Jesu"?' Abby suggested. 'I've sung it before but would be grateful for a reminder if you could print the sheet music.' Abby, a new member, could actually read music and brought up the general standard.

'"Little Donkey"?' Pippa offered. 'I could do a rap to go in the middle.'

'I could do "Silent Night" in Latvian?' Jade interjected.

'And I in Swedish,' Marli, a recent addition, added.

'And I can do the descant,' Karen said.

We decided on 'Joy to the World' along with a multi-language 'Silent Night'. I asked my musician husband if he could play the piano for us during the rehearsals and performance. For his part, he was keen to be able to see an area of my life that had hitherto been shut off; and for my part, he was the only musician I could find who would agree to do it for free. I negotiated a security check and gate pass for him.

Because of the upcoming performance we were given permission for choir members to take the afternoon off work for our final rehearsals. Jane, fresh from her performance of Governor Evil in the panto, ventured to join us for the final rehearsal and the performance, although she'd never sung in public.

'I can't fucking do this,' she said to a sympathetic Karen after the other six choir members who'd decided to join for the performance had shown her what would be required. Karen brought her a cup of coffee and she and Debs became Jane's chief encouragers.

'Don't worry if you get the tune wrong,' Debs said,

'just smile with all your teeth, put your hands on your hips and look like you never went wrong in the first place. It's all in the performance. If you act like it's right, they're not going to think it isn't.'

'I'll do the performance,' Jane concluded after the ups and downs of the rehearsal afternoon, 'but I'm not wearing the scarf.' The matching scarves had been made for us by the sewing sisters and she felt that the beige and gold chiffon did not contribute to the effect of her overall look.

They retired to the two reserved rows at the front of the chapel as we waited for the audience to take their seats. The Christmas service was a prison favourite so each row was filled and extra people stood leaning against the back wall. In anticipation of the event the chapel had been dressed by the Alpha group the afternoon before, so tinsel was draped across each window and handmade 'Merry Christmas' posters lined the walls. The chapel also had more natural light than anywhere else in the prison, by virtue of its unbarred windows. So as the choir filed onto the stage and arranged themselves in the order that we'd agreed upon, a strip of light fell diagonally across the composition. It was, I thought, a moment divine.

Everyone agreed the rendition of 'Silent Night', sung in three languages, was the highlight of the service. Lilly made it through the performance with Debs's hand steadying her if she wobbled off-note, and Jodie's clear, audible voice now sat comfortably among the others. Karen counted the scarves in at the end to make sure none had been siphoned off to the wings, the chapel emptied and Alice and I prepared to leave for Christmas.

I did not know then, but it would be the choir's last performance before I left the prison service the following August. By then the little social enterprise I'd helped to found before I got the job in the prison – a food waste café – would have grown to a size where it was able to employ me. Before long it would be able to support, host and help house women from the prison and other prisons around the region.

On my last day, we got together to sing for a final time. I'd eaten goodbye biscuits in the art sessions and been given homemade cards from our classes. I'd said my goodbyes by visiting cells along wing corridors and popping into offices, work parties and classrooms. I'd be back – covering lessons and visiting people who would be released and become part of the café family – but I would cease to be part of the fabric of the place, part of the day-to-day turning of prison life.

Like those leaving the prison as residents, I distributed my in-prison possessions – handing out the Pukka teabags to the group to drink and pass on to friends. We all said our thank yous and sang together our folk song warm-up: 'I'm going to lift my sister up, she is not heavy. If I don't lift my sister up, I will fall down.'

We ended with the choir favourite, 'Something Inside So Strong'. As the choir sang out the line 'the more you refuse to hear my voice, the louder I will sing' for the first time that day, my eyes filled. For all that I was given, and all the people's lives that I'd been privileged enough to share. And for all that they had taught me about strength in the face of adversity, and kindness in the face of fear.

DOUBLE BUBBLE

By Blacky

Do you want to know about the wheelings and dealings?
Do you know about two-for-one? I'll tell you about that.

Obviously now you can't get fags in jail but you used
to be able to. You used to get baccy. With two-for-one, if
you borrow a half-ounce you pay an ounce back. Lend
one out, get two back. So I had a baccy business going.
Me and two girls I was seeing. Not at the same time,
though, right? On two different sentences. One I had a
relationship with outside as well as in.

Anyway, remember, back then I was still on drugs,
so I'm in and out, in and out, wanting to come back
because, like I said, I felt I belonged. All those sentences
I was getting to know every little means and way to
get the clothes, money and drugs you need when you

haven't got anyone sending clothes or postal orders in. Right, it's like this: say you and me are both in jail now, Mim, and we're both on the gear. And I've just come in and I've got a fanny full of gear. Sorry for the swearing, but you're going to come to me, aren't you? And I'm going to get whatever I want for it 'cause you can't get it anywhere else. I'll do you a trade for it. I want an ounce of baccy off you, right? So then you'll get a wrap, and I'll have a stock of baccy.

For a long, long time I was doing that in the jail. Because we were doing that, there was a lot of baccy in our pad and a lot of other stuff – munch, toiletries. So if someone's without and they come for something then, yeah, I'll lend it, but whatever you got on your canteen, I want two back. Double bubble it's called.

It's called a business really, though, isn't it? That's what you call it. A baccy business or a munch business. Basically, whatever you lend, it's double back, unless it was your mate. If it was your mate, you'd lend her a half-ounce and get a half-ounce back. But, to a certain extent, who is your mate and who isn't your mate? 'Cause everyone's a mate, but no one's a mate, really. The only time you've met them is in jail. And everyone's in prison for doing something wrong so do you really trust them? But that's when loyalties come in, and that's where your head comes in.

You've got to have your wits about you in jail no

matter what. Always. And with your friends, or them you thinks is your friends. Even if you've lived with them on the streets. Doesn't matter. Jail's a different place. Even though everybody's like 'clean', nobody's 'clean'. That's how it goes.

EPILOGUE

Beyond the end of these pages, the lives I've written about continue to play out. Women continue to be held in a quarter wedge of the revolving door that they had often stepped into unawares as children or teens. The cycle of reoffending plods on, leaving in its wake the victims of crime. Addicts continue to fight for recovery. Fantastic officers and healthcare staff continue to join up and then, sometimes, to burn out. Doors and gates continue to be locked and unlocked, IEP warnings are given out and qualifications are earned for job markets that will be hard to crack.

And, for my part, working in prison has changed my life forever. The amazing people I met continue to be part of my daily life through our employability programmes at the café, our community church, and the small ethical tenancy project I helped to get going to provide housing for women – for now just a couple but hoping to grow. I continue to be so thankful for my safe, cosy house, and to share it through providing emergency accommodation in our spare room with NightStop.

But, most importantly, the experience continues to affect my life through friendships with amazing women. It's as a result of these friendships that I've attended more funerals in the last five years than in my previous 25 – mostly drug overdoses and drinking-related deaths. I've also had the privilege of seeing people rally round, carry on; I've heard incredible recovery stories and watched families reunited. We've had phone calls and camping trips and cups of tea and outings and painting groups.

I went into prison thinking that I would be able to teach women, and to reform a system. Instead, I learnt from those women and staff, and saw myself change.

But as these cycles of prison life continue, prison reform still sits at the bottom of our list of electoral priorities. I learnt very little in my politics and philosophy degree that I continue to use in my daily life, but this I did take away: that we do not persist with a broken framework for lack of other solutions. Howard Zehr, an American criminologist, writes: 'I have a dream that we won't have to talk about "restorative justice" because it will be understood that true justice is about restoration, and about transformation.'[16]

We need to change the narrative. To speak more firmly and more persistently than those whose shouting headlines and online rants would polarise us. Whose stories would say that we, the onlooker, are simply good and those in prison are simply bad. Whose narratives comfort us by making us believe that crime happens because there are bad people rather than making us reflect on the structural inequalities that mean that women in prison are statistically those who have drawn a bad ticket in life's lottery.

However unpleasant we make prisons, I can promise you that they will not suddenly become an effective deterrent to criminality. We will merely become like our American neighbours, whose prisons are exploitative and reoffending rates high, but who lock up more people than anyone else. Miserable prisons and lack of housing on release do not stop people committing crimes. They are a poor imitation of justice. Until we realise that we all contribute to the framework in which crimes are

---

[16] 'Howard Zehr's closing speech at the 2007 International Winchester Restorative Justice Conference', reported by: Brian Draper, 'Learning a Lesson from Moses', https://emu.edu/now/news/2008/01/learning-a-lesson-from-moses/ (accessed 28/12/18).

committed and all have an interest in the redemption, restoration and reintroduction into the community of those in the justice system, then we will continue to not make progress, and the people in prison will continue to be one of our country's dirty little secrets.

Those I've spoken to who are passionate about prison reform tend to have one thing in common: they know someone who's been to prison. They don't have the luxury of 'othering' prisoners. They don't talk of 'Mugger Mum' or 'Inmate A1435' or 'convicts', but of Lilly, Catherine and Nicki. My sincere hope in writing this book is that you now will too.

LESSONS (I LEARNT) FROM A WOMEN'S PRISON

Women are more brave, resilient and generous than you ever expect or imagine.

Crime doesn't happen in a vacuum.

More things are wrapped in foil than you might imagine. KitKats, yoghurt pots and everything made by Tunnock's. This is a problem for staff because we are not allowed to bring it into the prison, lest it be removed from the bin and used to take drugs.

Some people who live in prison look and sound like my grandma Jeanne and the people in her bridge club.

Prison staff are in constant need of a round of applause. They are superhuman and should be given medals, pay rises and extra colleagues.

I am utterly privileged and should be thankful every day for being housed, fed and relatively safe.

We should all be a little more horrified that everyone isn't housed, fed and relatively safe.

The dogs being taught to smell drugs learn new ones as they come out, like a canine software update.

Counselling is brilliant and we should all have some.

It is almost never beneficial to imprison women.

ACKNOWLEDGEMENTS

To list all of the people who have made *The Prison Teacher* happen would be impossible. Its existence was cheered on by a collective of friends, relatives and colleagues to whom I'm incredibly grateful.

Emily, my editor (and one of my best friends), is a good place to start. She wasn't only fantastic at making my words assemble together coherently but also gave me the confidence to write the book in the first place, and then stabilised my every wobble. Thank you too to the wonderful all-women power team – Virginia, Amy and Ru – who have been assembling the book and getting it into the right hands.

To Tom, Esther, Becca, Bex, Amy and Jessie, who made up our community house while I wrote it. They sat with me through tentative readings, made tea and prayed that it would get the sign off. And particularly to Nikki, who proof-read the whole book, laughed louder than was appropriate and cheer-led every chapter: to quote Ellie Goulding 'When I'm with you, I'm standing with an army'.

And to other exceptional humans who helped me keep my head above water while I was working in the prison and always: all of the Chandlers, Alice, Rory, Lois, Rob, Caitlin, Yas and Rich and my church community at St Johns; these people fed me and had me to stay and were shoulders to cry on in club toilets when I couldn't see much further than the previous day and the one ahead.

I am unbelievably blessed to have a family who love and support me even when they think I'm behaving irrationally. To Grandma and Catherine who read chapters through and who, no doubt, will get it on their book-club reading lists to increase sales. To my sisters, Ami and Naomi, who are pure gold and who build me up always. And to my mum – an incredible woman and inspiration – who gave me my faith and has an unwavering belief in my ability to change the world. I love her to pieces.

Huge appreciation is also due to my wonderful husband Sam (formerly the pianist from the choir chapter) who believes so unswervingly in me and my projects. The first draft of the book was due on our wedding day so in aid of getting it written he spent a lot of time on the phone to caterers and venues and relatives while I hibernated with my laptop.

My work with women was partially and now is fully funded by amazing sponsors: Helen, Wendy, Hillary, Ron and Ben. Obviously it would be nice if proper women's provision was state-funded, but it isn't, so three cheers for these wonderful humans who have stepped into the gap.

I can't name them here but I worked with an exceptional tiny team at the prison, particularly my two line managers who I compiled into 'Alice'. They are both still working in the charity and just absolutely radiate compassion from their bones. You know who you are.

Thanks to Gemma, Blacky, Vivian, Trish, and all the women at the Handcrafted arts group who wrote for the book and read through to keep it on track. Also a special mention to Michelle whose story of transformation constantly gives me reason to hope and whose support, along with Jose, I rely on so often in my work now. She is writing a book about her journey from prison to faith in God, which will be a much better read than this, so keep an eye out. Also to the Monday Night Group who help put fire in my belly and show me that strength sometimes looks like vulnerability and glory like failure.

And finally, to all those who I cannot name because they are still living inside, but who I remember so often for their kindness, strength and hope: thank you.

FURTHER READING
AND INFORMATION

If you'd like to find out more about prisons there are some amazing organisations and people that are worth googling and following:

Women In Prison: A campaign and research organisation – a great and very accessible place to start looking at some of the statistics.
@WIP_live www.womeninprison.org.uk

Michaela Booth: A blogger who is a former prisoner, criminology student and activist. Michaela should be the prison's policy adviser; honest and heartfelt.
@michaelabooth7 www.michaelamovement.blog

Prison Bag: A blog by a woman whose husband is in

prison. Really engaging stories about the experiences of partners and families. @prisonbag www.prisonbag.com

Prison Reform Trust: A good organisation to follow. They send a fab newsletter with good summaries of research and policy, etc.
@PRTuk www.prisonreformtrust.org.uk

Open Clasp Theatre: A theatre company that makes amazing collaborative theatre in prisons. See anything they do if you ever get the chance.
@OpenClasp www.openclasp.org.uk

Koestler Trust: An organisation which hosts awards and exhibition for art from prison; catch an exhibition if you can!
@KoestlerTrust www.koestlertrust.org.uk

David Breakspear: David has spent time in prison and is now studying for a criminology degree. He's a positive and hopeful voice about what's needed. @areformed-man www.journeyofareformedman.net

Faith Spear: A criminologist. She is well-connected with lots of people in the criminal justice conversation so it's a great feed for keeping up to date on current conversations. @fmspear

Junction 42: A brilliant prison chaplaincy and arts organisation in the north east. If you're interested in how to do great chaplaincy on both sides of the gate then they have a fantastic model. @junction_42

Lucy Baldwin: Author of mothering justice (see below) and all-round wise woman on working with women in social work, healthcare and justice. @lucybaldwin08

The Howard League: A research and campaigning body. They produce some great studies. @thehowardleague

Richard W Hardwick, *The Truth About Prisons: Prisonsers, Professionals and Families Speak Out* (Northumberland, 2017): A fantastic book which compiles stories from prison residents, staff and families.
@RWHardwick www.thetruthaboutprison.com

Baz Dreisinger, *Incarceration Nations* (Other Press, 2017): A trip around the world voting different prisons and comparing different approaches to criminal justice.

Dr Lucy Baldwin, *Mothering Justice* (Waterside Press, 2015): A must-read for anyone working with women, and very readable if, like me, you struggle to get through wordy research.

The Secret Barrister, *The Secret Barrister* (Picador, 2018): This book showed me some of the reasons why the system is putting the wrong people inside.

Sophie Campbell, *Breakfast at Bronzefield* (Sophie Campbell Books, 2020): A personal account from Sophie Campbell about her time in Bronzefield prison. Gritty, profound, beautiful and about bloody time someone published a woman who's been in prison. @sophieCbooks

Chris Atkins, *A Bit of a Stretch* (Atlantic, 2020). A funny and harrowing account of a men's prison from a man who never expected to be inside.

Lucy Baldwin and Ben Raikes ed., *Seen and Heard* (Waterside Press, 2019). A compilation of work from children and parents affected by imprisonment.

ABOUT THE AUTHOR

Mim Skinner runs the women's project for the charity Handcrafted, supporting women to connect to community, housing and recovery through creativity. She also is a co-founder and director of multi-award-winning community interest company RE^{F}USE, which works to intercept food that would otherwise go to landfill. In the last six months they've redirected 27 tonnes of food to bellies not bins. The RE^{F}USE café in Chester-Le-Street also provides supported volunteering opportunities for those with barriers to employment such as addiction or poor mental health, working alongside probation and local mental health services. Mim lives in the north-east of England with her husband, Sam and their cat, Monkey.